EDDY
MERCKX
OUT ON HIS OWN

EDDY MERCKX

OUT ON HIS OWN

GUY ROGER

TRANSLATED BY ROLAND HALL

BLOOMSBURY SPORT

LONDON · OXFORD · NEW YORK · NEW DELHI · SYDNEY

BLOOMSBURY SPORT
Bloomsbury Publishing Plc
50 Bedford Square, London, WC1B 3DP, UK
Bloomsbury Publishing Ireland Limited,
29 Earlsfort Terrace, Dublin 2, D02 AY28, Ireland

BLOOMSBURY, BLOOMSBURY SPORT and the Diana logo are trademarks of
Bloomsbury Publishing Plc

First published in 2024 in the French language as *Inaccessible Merckx*
© 2024, Editions Solar, an imprint of Edi8, Paris, France
First published in Great Britain 2026

For legal purposes the Acknowledgements on p. 291
constitute an extension of this copyright page

A catalogue record for this book is available from the British Library

Library of Congress Cataloguing-in-Publication data has been applied for

ISBN: HB: 978-1-3994-3000-5; eBook: 978-1-3994-2997-9

2 4 6 8 10 9 7 5 3 1

Typeset in Bembo Std by Lumina Datamatics Ltd
Printed and bound in Great Britain by Clays Ltd, Elcograf S.p.A.

To find out more about our authors and books visit www.bloomsbury.com
and sign up for our newsletters
For product safety related questions contact productsafety@bloomsbury.com

CONTENTS

Thévenet (L) and Merckx (C) escape during the 15th stage of
the Tour de France between Nice and Pra-Loup on 13 July, 1975

PREFACE BY BERNARD THÉVENET

Eddy Merckx started the Tour de France seven times. He won five and I won the other two. It was a long time before I realised that I had been the first to dethrone him, because Merckx was – is – a phenomenon. He was a one-of-a-kind rider, who won when he wanted to. For me, an amateur rider at the cycling club Athletic Club de Boulogne-Billancourt (ACBB), he was like a creature from another planet. In our room at the Bataillon de Joinville (the sports regiment of the French military), Bernard Dupuch, Charly Rouxel, Jean-Jacques Sanquer and I put up a poster of him crossing the finish line at the 1967 UCI Road World Championships in Heerlen. I can still see it to this day. He beat Jan Janssen (world champion in 1964) by just a few centimetres in that sprint… The sheer power he had was extraordinary.

He and I were rivals but not enemies. I've never seen a rider who was so hungry for victory yet so loyal. He was ruthless but fair, and when it came to the yellow jersey he was no different. I always got on well with old Eddy. I was not even a reserve for the Peugeot team slated to ride the Tour in 1970, the year I made my first professional appearance in cycling. But when Ferdinand Bracke, holder of the hour record (1967) and Gerben Karstens, the Dutch

National Champion in 1966, withdrew at the last minute, it meant our *directeur sportif*, Gaston Plaud, had little choice. I never knew why he called me to be 10th man. Maybe it was because I lived not far from Limoges, where the Tour started that year. Two weeks later, on 14 July, I won the stage at La Mongie. I remember the next day in the press, Merckx said, 'He's going to be good. We'll be seeing him again in a year or two.' At the age of 22 that kind of compliment – from a yellow jersey winner – stays with you for your whole career, beyond even.

I was on the Tour again the following year, for the famous Merckx–Ocaña duel. In the climb up to Orcières, Ocaña, a Spanish road racer who'd won the Vuelta a España in 1970, was way ahead. Merckx and I were in a group of chasers. We were seven minutes behind. I could have taken a turn up front but I didn't, I was too worried about being dropped. At one point we were side by side, and Eddy said to me, 'You got anything left to drink?' I gave him my bottle. It was a way of making up for my lack of effort. I doubt he remembers that detail.

In 1975, a few Tours later, I won the yellow jersey in Pra-Loup. During the night, I got up to go to the bathroom. The shutters in my room were open, and the moonlight was shining on the yellow jersey on the back of a chair. I remember saying to myself, 'Why did Eddy leave his yellow jersey in my room?' I saw first-hand how a victory in the Tour de France changes your life and how people see you.

At a post-Tour criterium in Château-Chinon after the 1974 Tour, I had won a Paris–Nice stage and Merckx had won his fifth Tour de France. President François Mitterrand came over to greet us. He shook my hand for about a second. But when he got to Merckx he wouldn't let go. At the same post-Tour criterium in 1975, Mitterrand was there again. This time he shook my hand for a full five minutes. It was all about the yellow jersey!

Eddy and I still see each other when the old riders meet up, or at other events. We share the same passion, and it's not going to let go of us now. Passion always comes before a fight. We chat about everything, nothing, the riders of today and tomorrow. But there's one topic we never touch on: defeat. It's too painful. For him as much as it is for me. We call that respect. I am proud to have had him as an opponent, and even prouder to have earned his respect.

Eddy formally announces his retirement on 18 May, 1978 © AP Photo/Pierre Thielemans

KEMZEKE, EAST FLANDERS: 19 MARCH, 1978: THE FINAL RACE

'Pierrot, it's over. I'm stopping. Don't tell anyone, but that was my last race.'

EDDY MERCKX

In March 1978, no small degree of excitement took hold of the small town of Kemzeke, next to Saint Nicolas, in East Flanders, Belgium. The Tour of Flanders was starting from there in less than a month. It was the only subject of discussion over a few beers in the Café De Linde. It seemed that in only a few days' time, Eddy Merckx would be starting the Omloop van het Waasland (the Waasland circuit). The Belgian champion had had a tumultuous winter. Instead of training he had been glued to his phone, trying to get a new sponsor.

At the last minute, C&A clothing stores came to the rescue following the abrupt withdrawal of Wilkinson razor blades. Everything had been ready – shirts, shorts, bikes, race calendar – when the French razor manufacturer pulled out and it was back to the drawing board. To reassure his team,

Eddy Merckx paid the salaries of the 18 riders using his own money. That included Robert Mintkiewicz, seven-time rider in the Tour de France and the only Frenchman on the team. It was no secret that at the start of his 14th season the five-time winner of the Tour de France was out of shape, and his health problems did not inspire confidence. He had dropped out three times in four races between 19 February and 11 March: Montauroux, Het Volk and Wilsele. His fifth place in the Tour du Haut Var was a pale reflection of his usual form. Under those conditions, there was no way he was going to be part of the line-up for the Milan–San Remo, which was 288km long that year.

Sunday 19 March was a grey spring day that felt more like autumn. Roger De Vlaeminck, nicknamed 'The Gypsy', had triumphed in *La Primavera* the day before. Ignoring all the problems that could affect him, Merckx was there at the start of the Omloop van het Waasland. The race organisers had given him bib number 4. It was the first time that Merckx, very much a household name by then, had taken part, and his presence gave an unexpected dimension to the event long organised by Dancing Ponderosa before it opened up to professionals. In his race review for the Flemish magazine *Bahamontes* at the time, journalist Rik Van Puymbroeck quoted from the event's official accounts: 'Of the total prize fund of 101,500 Belgian francs (the equivalent of £2215), Mr Merckx received a sum of 30,000 Belgian francs (£656).'

It was cold, and rain showers made the cobblestones slippery. Rough, uneven cobbles that catch and the howling Belgian wind made it a race for the strong of heart. Merckx's Mercedes, driven by his friend and *soigneur*

Pierrot De Wit, was engulfed as soon as he cut the igni-
tion. The start and finish line below the gloomy town hall
was only 100 yards away but it was a struggle to reach
it. The church square was far too small for the bustling,
sentimental crowd in thrall of their idol. If they could,
people would have kissed his hands and feet as he passed.
An observer – one José De Cauwer in bib number 65, who
later made waves in his Ti-Raleigh jersey – was mesmer-
ised: 'Knowing him, it is impossible that he didn't say to
himself, in the middle of all that fuss, "What the hell am
I doing here?"'

And then there was the question of the prowling pack
of photographers, taking pictures of him from every angle,
making it feel like the end of an era. A long time afterwards,
De Cauwer did confess, 'That we didn't exist came as no
surprise, but harassing him that much was positively inde-
cent.' In his article entitled 'When Merckx was Merckx
no Longer,' Van Puymbroeck noted the following detail:
'To protect themselves from the cold wind, the racers had
long sleeves and wore caps under their sausage helmets.' He
also interviewed René Dillen, Merckx's teammate at C&A:
'Just before the start Eddy was alone, and cut off from the
rest of the competitors because of all the supporters who
were hounding him. I've never used my elbows as much as
I did that day, to get him to the line. I knew it was going
to be a bad day.' And yet this suffering became an inner
force, and rather than crushing him, it gave him a new and
terrible strength.

At 1 p.m. the race organisers released the 65 competitors, who'd been standing around for a good while. As
soon as the flag went down, Dillen shot off. He had gained

a small lead of maybe 30 seconds or so. 'When I turned to see what the gap was, who should I see riding hard at the front of the peloton? Eddy.' Merckx was Merckx. Even when he wasn't at his best he was still a tireless fighter. He even managed a little breakaway an hour into the race and opened up a little distance... That is how he liked to ride. All in – all the time! But sometimes giving your all is not enough, and by mid-race he was back in the pack. 'There was no question of doing him any favours,' said De Cauwer. 'He certainly never did any for anyone else. And the guys were racing their Milan–San Remo against Merckx, and all they could think about was taking him down.' The 1978 leaderboard shows Frans Van Looy as the winner, ahead of Walter Planckaert after a hard sprint to the finish. Merckx came in a few seconds later, in a small group of about 10 riders. At stake was an 11th-place finish that José De Cauwer snatched from him. 'I had never seen him up so close. We were shoulder to shoulder 200m from the finish line and I beat him in the sprint. I will remember it until the end of my days.'

What came next was more emotional. Pierrot De Wit, known as 'Goldfinger' by generations of riders on the circuit, including Maspes, Faggin, Timoner, Van Steenbergen, Koblet, Darrigade, Sercu and Doyle, was Eddy's *soigneur* and masseur. He said, 'I had just finished washing down his legs with a glove. He got up, closed the door, and said to me, really calmly, "Pierrot, it's over. I'm stopping. Don't tell anyone, but that was my last race. No Tour of Belgium. I won't go any further." I tried to tell him that it wasn't as bad as all that, but he was just shaking his head. "No, Pierrot, I've suffered enough. It's over."' It remained a secret for a few days, but then the normal world that Eddy had left behind in 1965 came back to him like a boomerang.

Forty-six years later, the story of the 1978 Waasland circuit resurfaced, thanks to José De Cauwer. He was a commentator at BRT, the Dutch-speaking Belgian TV channel, after being *directeur sportif* of the ADR team and the main instigator of American road racer Greg LeMond's victory over Laurent Fignon in the 1989 Tour de France – the most famous eight seconds in cycling history.

De Cauwer had written, with journalist Rik Van Walleghem, the book he had always wanted to write. It was called *10 Geboden van José De Cauwer* (José De Cauwer's 10 Commandments) and it was a roaring success. Merckx and LeMond featured prominently, and the work shed light on some aspects of riders' lives that are rarely discussed. When I made an appointment to see him I had no idea if he would reveal anything about Eddy Merckx's last race, which features prominently in his 10 Commandments.

In a café-bookshop in Gent, near the Sint-Pieters train station, José doesn't stop talking. We learn that he is 'part of his inner circle,' that 'Merckx the man is a faithful reflection of the rider, but is more sentimental,' and that a 'kid like me had the privilege of beating him in a sprint, although it was only for 11th place.' The two authors had great success when they went out on the road and made public appearances, where they discussed not only the book but what went on behind the scenes. De Cauwer and Van Walleghem, accompanied by a guitarist who filled the interval with his tunes, travelled from town to town and from hall to community centre across their flat country. They soon made it to 50 appearances. All the while embellishing the tales and letting themselves get caught up in the questions from the audience. De Cauwer came out with a few personal insights: 'By the time I was 14, I was already working a 50-hour week in a foundry.' Courage and humility were the foundations of his career, during which his close friendship with Hennie Kuiper (one of the only riders to have won both the Olympic and World professional road races) transformed him into a *domestique* (support rider). 'In this business, I thought more often about survival than victory (one stage of the 1976 Vuelta a España) and, by listening and watching, I realised there were two things you should never talk about: good luck and bad luck. The first, because what happens to you is never down to luck. The second, because if you are looking for excuses, you'll never win.'

In his 10 Commandments, he recounts with great sensitivity and humour the day of 19 March, 1978 – the great Eddy Merckx's final race. The first thing he said, with a tone of regret and a voice full of emotion, was, 'If we had known how much we would miss him we would have appreciated him more at the time.' In their public performances the two writers imagined Eddy's return home that day, where Claudine, his wife, was waiting for him:

> *Eddy:* You'll never guess what's happened now?
> *Claudine:* No. Did your last race go well?
> *Eddy:* (After a pause) De Cauwer beat me in a sprint... (another pause) for 11th place.
> *Claudine:* Then it's definitely time to think about stopping for good.

The public laughed, sales soared. It is undeniable: a full half-century after his career ended, Eddy Merckx is still a formidable presence in the collective imagination.

Long-time friends Eddy and José still meet up occasionally for a meal. In mid-December 2023, the announced closure of the famous Hof Van Cleve restaurant in Kruishoutem – three Michelin stars, 19.5/20 from food critics Henri Gault and Christian Millau – gave them a suitable pretext for a meet. Chef Peter Goossens sat them at the best, most requested table – the one closest to the kitchen. Eight days later King Philippe of Belgium had lunch in the very same spot. Between courses, the subject of De Cauwer's 10 Commandments came up, in particular the imaginary scene of the warrior's return home and the ensuing conversation with his wife, as described above.

'And?' I asked, 'how did he take it?'

'Eddy creased up.'

*Vincennes, 1969: Merckx arriving at the final
stage for his first Tour de France victory*

WOLUWE-SAINT-PIERRE: THE ORIGIN OF A CYCLING GENIUS

'Eddy Merckx was the main attraction. Next to
him we were only bit-part players.'

FRANS VERBEECK

To find yourself on the starting line of a book devoted
to the greatest race cyclist of all time is a monumental
adventure, the heady feeling of embarking on a world
tour from a time when cycling still really meant something to people.

From the 1960s to the 1970s, Eddy Merckx left his mark
on nearly every race he was in. The statistics indicate he
took part in 1800 races, with 525 victories. It's a formidable return from a 14-year career. It's a performance
made all the more remarkable by the fact that at that time
and in every way, the opposition was significant, giving
rise to some fascinating duels. It is amazing that Merckx,
the most voracious 'Cannibal' that cycling has ever
known, breathed the same invigorating air as Roger De
Vlaeminck, Walter Godefroot, Freddy Maertens, Roger
Rosiers, André Dierickx, Frans Verbeeck, Patrick Sercu,

Jan Janssen, Felice Gimondi, Luis Ocaña, Gianni Motta, Lucien Van Impe, Joop Zoetemelk, Bernard Thévenet and Rik Van Looy.

A list of his many achievements would give you enough material to write a beginner's guide to cycle racing. From Vilvoorde, his first success (11 May, 1965), to Kluisbergen, his last (17 September, 1977), newcomers to the sport would learn all about many of the most iconic locations in cycling's international heritage. The Poggio, Muro di Sormano, Passeo del Ghisallo, the Grammont Wall, the Oude Kwaremont, the Trouée d'Arenberg, the Carrefour de l'Arbre, Stockeu and the Côte de la Redoute are just a few. And there's a special mention for Woluwe-Saint-Pierre, the part of Brussels where Merckx grew up, and that he put on the world map.

Perhaps because Belgium had been desperately waiting for a successor to Sylvère Maes – their last winner of the Tour de France, in 1939 – the arrival of Eddy Merckx to the international cycling scene was akin to lighting the blue touchpaper on a firework. He rapidly became a riding – and winning – machine. Day and night, constantly crossing international borders, Eddy did not rest from one year to the next. He would start with a criterion in Brussels in the morning, fly to Lisbon and win a second crit in the late afternoon, then fly to Milan and end the day with a Madison at the Velodromo Vigorelli. According to former journalist Rik Van Walleghem, during his journey in professional cycling, 'Eddy the Explorer' would have circumvented the globe around 12 times. 'In his own way, he conquered space on a human-propulsion machine,' said Jean-Baptiste Baronian.[1] It is a thought echoed by Frans Verbeeck, another classy consumer of cobbles: 'Eddy Merckx was the main attraction. Next to him we were only bit-part players.'

Peter Post, *directeur sportif* of the Raleigh team, put it another way the evening after Merckx's display in the 1973 Paris–Roubaix: 'Why on earth does the Belgian Prime Minister Vanden Boeynants need to buy Mirages or F16s when he already has Merckx?'[2]

You can't take anything away from the huge seasons he raced, some of which had more than 160 days of racing. And this should be taken in context with some of his other outstanding feats: Mourenx-Ville-Nouvelle, Tre Cime di Lavaredo, Mendrisio and Mexico are the places legends were made. In fact, Merckx's career should be looked at as whole, as one would look at a Flemish landscape by Brueghel or Rubens, complete with mountains, snow, thunderstorms, gusts of wind and cobblestones.

Evoking the 'god of gods and his Babylonian prize list', Baronian quotes French playwright Alfred Jarry, who long before the birth of the *monstre sacré* (sacred monster), had already asserted that 'cycling, this sport at the limit of sport, is one of the Beaux Arts.' The artist Merckx thus elevated his work to be with the greatest of all time, in the image of his illustrious predecessors such as Binda, Coppi, Bartali, Bobet and Anquetil, as well as those of the generation that followed: Thévenet, Hinault, Induráin, Froome and Pogačar. I'm tempted to add that the Belgian champion

[1] *Dictionnaire Amoureux de la Belgique* (Dictionary for Lovers of Belgium), 2015, Baronian
[2] *Dans l'Ombre d'Eddy Merckx* (In the Shadow of Eddy Merckx), 2012, Johny Vansevenant

had something that none of those others did: he made a reality of the fantastic. 'Because he had one immutable thing: a truly extraordinary degree of willpower. It was a guiding principle for him,' says the cycling historian Pascal Sergent, author of many books on cycling in Belgium from that decade.

Merckx is so well known in Belgium that he is considered as a social phenomenon, not simply a sportsman. Robert Janssens, author and former journalist of the newspaper *Het Laatste Nieuws*, and who is an authority on Eddy's career, says, 'The Merckx name has even acquired an educational dimension through its presence in schools.' He also goes on to say, 'Merckx is part of the Belgian national heritage. He is like an ambassador of pride for all Belgians, and each new generation tells of his legend, thereby perpetuating it. That legend lives in the hearts of an entire nation.' Retracing the Merckx years involves diving into the social history of cycling. In his masterful book *The World of Yesterday* (1942), the Austrian writer Stefan Zweig noted: 'Under normal circumstances, the name a human being bears is no more than the band is to a cigar: a means of identification, a superficial, almost unimportant thing that is only loosely related to the real subject, the true ego.' He continued: 'In the event of a success the name begins to swell, so to say. It loosens itself from the human being that bears it and becomes a power in itself, a force, an independent thing, an article of commerce, a capital asset; and psychologically again with strong reaction it becomes a force which tends to influence, to dominate, to transform the person who bears it.' The name of Pelé, the world's most famous football star and the greatest player of all time, is the perfect illustration of this phenomenon. 'He could stop a war by his presence alone, or convert America to soccer,' Stéphane Cohen said in his excellent biography.[3]

As for Merckx, his influence hasn't quite reached the level of Pelé's yet, but it is certain that the Belgian champion's name has long surpassed the man himself. A Metro station bears his name (Line 5, Brussels) and there are films (*La Course en Tête* by Joël Santoni; *American Flyers* by John Badham; *Le Vélo de Ghislain Lambert* by Philippe Harel), songs (Jacques Higelin, Group Sttela), graphic novels (*San Antonio*; *Asterix in Belgium*), an educational centre (Woluwe-Saint-Pierre), the velodrome in Gent, popularly known as the 'Eddy Merckx', and many statues and monuments all serve as confirmation.

The five-time winner of the Tour de France is also the rider about whom the most has been written. There are 82 books about him in French on the shelves of the BNF[4] in Paris. There are more than 100 written in Dutch; they can be found in KOERS, the Museum of Cycle Racing in Roeselare, Belgium. Amazon lists page after page of English-language volumes about him; translations and originals. And that is all without talking of the unprecedented media whirlwind that blew during and after his career.

On 18 May, 1978, the day of Eddy's farewell, journalist Lucien Berghmans – who had been tasked with writing about the champion every day (and that meant *every* day, without exception) for 14 years – 'was far more concerned about what *he* was going to do than about Merckx's

---

[3] *Pelé*, 2023, Stéphane Cohen
[4] Bibliothèque Nationale de France (the National Library of France)

retirement,' reports Rik Van Puymbroeck in the magazine *Bahamontes*.

The goal of this book is not to retell the story of a historical figure. That has already been done, and done well. Nor is this an intimate journey into the story of his life. The biography by the Belgian political journalist Johny Vansevenant is a must-read; it is remarkable in every way.

A whole generation – an entire era – lives and breathes in those 14 seasons. Sometimes it is dressed up with a veneer of romance, but The Cannibal's escapes and crazy escapades are brought to life in the memories of his adversaries and companions along the way. At random: Gianni Motta, his whipping-boy in the Milan–San Remo: 'He was everything we dreamed of being and becoming. The trouble was that sometimes it felt like we were riding behind a motorbike!'

Jean-Pierre Danguillaume, Bernard Thévenet's right-hand man: 'It was like a boxing match between a lightweight and a heavyweight. Did you ever see Cassius Clay get beaten by a lightweight?'

Jean-Claude Genty, Luis Ocaña's teammate: 'In the races in Belgium, us Frenchmen were all over the place. During that time Eddy Merckx and Roger De Vlaeminck were having the time of their lives!'

Roger Rosiers, winner of the 1971 Paris–Roubaix: 'As soon as he took the lead, you knew something was going to happen. I have never seen someone with such pure power.'

These are the faces, the characters who tell the story of an era; that of the Rolling Stones and Bob Dylan, of *Apollo 11* and Pelé's Brazil, who became world champions for the third time in 1970. Everywhere I went, Belgium, Italy, the Netherlands, Spain, France, every meeting with these glorious old-timers – these elite riders – was exceptional. They gave me little nuggets, secret stories and even shed a few tears. Just dive in and help yourself.

But first, a brief personal observation: Eddy Merckx did not directly influence my passion for cycling, and I can't say I was a 'Merckxist'. Years after he stopped riding, I interviewed him. Once after an outing to accompany his son Axel, who was eager to follow in his father's pedals (what flows in the blood is as difficult to divert as the course of the Thames), and again with his Thursday mates. But I never saw him race until I came across some images in the INA[5] archives. Many of them were in black and white, but they were breathtaking. It was fascinating how they transported you back to another time. And that is how I came to learn about the real life of Eddy Merckx the cyclist.

While researching and writing, I often asked myself the following two questions: Is he the greatest cyclist of all time? What makes his character so compelling? My response to the second question was always the same: I always found him noble, courageous and dignified in those old films in the INA. Merckx was not only an outstanding champion unlike any other, he is an institution. And that is the answer to my first question. And the overwhelming majority of the testimonies I heard confirmed it.

[5]Institut Nationale de l'Audiovisuel (France's National Audiovisual Institute)

Merckx during the 1969 Tour de France, which he went on to win

LA CIPALE, ONCE:
TOUR DE FRANCE, 1969

'Taking the lead at Tourmalet ... that's a moment that stays with you for life. As climbers, we all have those peaks that bring a special kind of pride and emotion.'

MARTIN VAN DEN BOSSCHE, TEAMMATE

The Tour de France is the foundation of Merckxism. The 1969 Tour was Eddy Merckx's first close encounter with cycling's ultimate race. It had fascinated him from childhood, when he had dreamed about his idol, the Belgian sprint cyclist Stan Ockers. And the Tour remains the event that made the greatest impression on his life. He was so keen on the race that even before he earned the nickname 'The Cannibal', customers at the grocer's shop in the Place des Bouvreuils (run by Merckx's parents Jenny and Jules), called him 'Tour de France'.

The 1969 Tour de France – the first of his five wins – is probably the most outstanding. He obliterated the competition after only a week. At the end of the Tour, Roger Pingeon, in second, was 17 minutes and 54 seconds behind him. Raymond Poulidor, third, was 22 minutes and 13 seconds behind, and Jan Janssen – the previous year's winner – was 10th, some 52 minutes and 56 seconds behind. In the first of his 15 entries, Lucien Van Impe finished 56 minutes and 17 seconds behind the leader. As for Luis Ocaña, he dropped out at the start of the second week.

It was an utterly decisive win: yellow jersey, six stage victories, green jersey for points classification, King of the Mountains, leader in combativity. His Italian team, Faema, was the only one to reach Paris in its entirety and won the team rankings. Eddy's obsession with setting up what was pretty much a commando team – 20 guys all ready to put themselves on the line for him – finally paid off. It was a long way from the days when he had to suffer at the hands of Rik Van Looy, his team leader at Solo-Superia, where he made his professional debut in 1965. Long gone was the selfish behaviour of Tom Simpson and Roger Pingeon, the leaders of the Peugeot team: 'In two years, I can't recall a single team-mate ever giving me a wheel or taking a pull at the front.'[6] Merckx was 23 when the upheavals of May 1968[7] crossed into Belgium, but he didn't need that to know what he wanted: to overthrow the old order of the Van Looy generation. He did it his own way, which was rarely the easiest. His character was such that he wouldn't fall into line, blindly following orders. He would never have settled for the role of *domestique*.

His first campaign in Italy in 1968 demonstrated this perfectly: he added a Giro and a Paris–Roubaix to his already impressive win list which had a World Championship (1967)

---

[6] *Face à Face avec Eddy Merckx* (Face to Face with Eddy Merckx), 1971, Marc Jeuniau
[7] May 1968 saw unrest from general strikes in France cross the border into Belgium, where Flemish students at the University of Leuven demanded a split between the Dutch and French-speaking divisions of the University, creating a countrywide linguistic and political crisis.

and two Milan–San Remos (1966, 1967) on it already. It was further bolstered after his 1969 Classics campaign, when he added a third Milan–San Remo, a Tour of Flanders, a Liège–Bastogne–Liège, a Gent–Wevelgem (now known as In Flanders Fields – from Middelkerke to Wevelgem), a Flèche Wallonne and a Paris–Nice. Merckx did brilliantly to entrust Belgian National Road Race Champion (1966) Guido Reybrouck with the mission of finding teammates in his image: hard-working, supportive, loyal and who would form a perfectly cohesive group. 'No Dutch!' warned the boss. Message understood. Twelve Belgians started the Italian adventure in the 1968 season. It lasted nine years. The Italian directors made up the membership of the first Faema team with six of their own countrymen.

However, the two clans were at odds with each other pretty quickly. The Italians rode for Vittorio Adorni, but the Belgians were giving their all for Eddy Merckx. Adorni, who had won the Giro d'Italia in 1965, was team leader for the 1968 Vuelta a España. Eddy Merckx would be afforded the same privilege in the Giro a month later. But on the road in Spain nothing went as planned, and an obscure manoeuvre by Adorni caused a fracture in the group. In an editorial, Martin Van Den Bossche, who Tour de France director Jacques Goddet once made his 'mountain lieutenant', came out with the following accusation: 'Adorni betrayed us. I saw it with my own eyes.'

I went to meet the veteran mountain specialist whose 'legs never tired' (another quote from Jacques Goddet), at his home in Bornem, located halfway between Brussels and Antwerp. Robert Janssens, a writer who was with *Het Laatste Nieuws* as a journalist for 40 years, was with me. 'At the time there were two rival factions, and they weren't even talking to each other,' Van Den Bossche told us. 'But we had a job to do, and that was keeping an eye out for Gimondi, our main competitor, who was riding for the Salvarani team. In truth, it was all a charade. On the big mountain stage, Gimondi went on the attack and I started to follow. Right at that moment Adorni grabbed my jersey and held me back. And that's how Gimondi won the Vuelta a España. That evening at the dinner table I asked Adorni a question in Flemish, even though he didn't understand the language. But I made sure he knew what I was talking about by rubbing my index finger and thumb together as I spoke: "Hey! How much did you get?" I said, adding, "you'd better share what you got with those of us who have been riding with you since the start or it won't go well when I tell Eddy that you sold us out on the Vuelta." Straight away, Marino Vigna, our *directeur sportif*, jumped in. He was pointing his finger at me, trying to scare me: "I can tell you right now that you'll be watching the next Giro on television." But Eddy was in charge, so I was there at the start of the 1968 Giro. He must have thought he'd done well to select me when we hit the snowstorm on the way to the Tre Cime di Lavaredo.'

Little did Merckx know that in the following Giro, during which he absolutely crushed all-comers, he would be the victim of the greatest injustice of his life. In Savona, after two weeks, he was kicked out of the race. He had tested positive for Fencamfamine, a stimulant of the Reactivan family, and was suspended for a month. 'It was the biggest stitch-up I've ever seen,' sighed Van Den Bossche, who shared a room with the pink jersey winner of that Giro d'Italia. 'Seriously, if you only knew what doping control was like at the finish... Some kind of mobile laboratory where the *tifosi* (fans or supporters) could come and go as they pleased. There were a dozen people in there who had nothing to do with anything. The urine samples were not even sealed in front of us. Anyone could have put anything in a test tube. As far as I'm concerned, Savona was revenge.' It went all the way to the top: questions were asked in the Belgian parliament. The suspension was eventually lifted, in light of multiple procedural errors, and Merckx was in Roubaix for the start of his first Tour de France on 28 June, 1969.

On the list of participants, the Faema team selected only one Italian rider, Pietro Scandelli. It looked like the lesson of the 1968 Vuelta had been learned. The other eight were all pure-bred Flemish who had signed an ironclad pact. It was like the Knights of the Round Table. Mintjens, Reybrouck, Spruyt, Stevens, Swerts, Vandenberghe, Van Schil and Van Den Bossche, all of whom were flawless, and who bossed the peloton for three weeks. 'At Faema, everyone had a precise, unchanging role, which meant that there was no room for improvisation or the slightest surprise. My speciality was the mountains,' said Martin Van Den Bossche. However, something did happen internally that left a shadow over Merckx's overwhelming domination of the Tour for a very long time.

Back to the Tour, 15 July, 1969: On the climb up to Tourmalet, the sun was beating down hard on the riders' backs. More than 50 years separate this stage in the Pyrenees from my visit to Martin Van Den Bossche on one of those cold, rainy mornings that would never stop a Flemish cyclist from going for a ride. The many hours spent hunched over a bike have not lessened his enthusiasm. Nor have the 70-hour weeks it has taken to launch his small tile import-export business. The business, now run by his son, spreads out over more than 18,000 square metres. But the conversation quickly returns to the 1969 Tour. The day after Raymond Delisle's stage win on Bastille Day – the French champion's jersey on his shoulders – the Faema team took a firm grip on the Tour. At the base of Tourmalet, Van Den Bossche took the lead. He knew when he turned around that Merckx was right behind him so, as was his wont, turn after turn he increased the pace, again and again, 'until I could no longer hear anyone talking or grumbling in the small breakaway group. Then I realised that it was just the two of us, me and Eddy. We were getting close to the summit and I was going to take the lead at Tourmalet. A moment that stays with you for life. As climbers, we all have those peaks that bring a special kind of pride and emotion. For me, it was Tourmalet. I thought I had him beaten, but 200m from the banner Eddy pulled out – he didn't look back. He dropped me cold and quickly vanished on the descent.'

Disappointed, Van Den Bossche eased off and was caught by a small chasing pack, while the yellow jersey raced away in what will remain one of the great pages of glory in his career. 'It was nothing but madness, a marvellous and noble madness,' the writer Stefan Zweig could have said had he witnessed the audacious move, 140km from the finish.

The next day in *L'Équipe*, Merckx was referred to as 'Merckxissimo' by Jacques Goddet. The journalist dared, for the first time, to draw a comparison with *Il Campionissimo*, the unforgettable Fausto Coppi: 'What Eddy Merckx is doing I have never witnessed before. Even in his prime, Fausto Coppi never contested a Tour in this way. Merckx will stand alone in the annals of cycling sport. This is the 35th Tour I have seen and I had to wait until now to discover the perfect team leader. How many generations will be able to produce a new Merckx? The only downside to such a phenomenon is that it reduces everyone else to the role of an extra. It is the first time in the history of cycling that we have seen such an outstanding individual talent. Merckx doesn't simply dominate his generation, he's in a different league.'

At Mourenx-Ville-Nouvelle, the first group to come in, of which Van Den Bossche was part, was 7 minutes and 46 seconds behind. 'I let Dancelli have second place in exchange for 20 good tyres,' Martin smiled.

That evening at the hotel, he was still reeling from the day's events. He was still turning it all over in his mind when he went past Merckx's room and – without thinking – knocked on the door. Martin can still see himself saying, 'Today, as the faithful *domestique*, I just hoped for some small gesture from a great champion such as yourself.' But, by replaying that scene over the past few days, Van Den Bossche finally understood.

A few days later, the Italian Marino Basso, a sprinter who rode for team Molteni, told Eddy that the boss, Pietro Molteni – the 'salami king' – wanted to take him on for a salary four times higher than Faema. 'To be honest, I did have a few words to say to Eddy about it. He just replied that there was a Tour de France to win, but he took offence, I could tell.' Van Den Bossche even told us that at the end of the Tour, Jean Van Buggenhout, a central figure in Merckx's affairs and the tough manager who helped shape cycling in Belgium and elsewhere, 'summoned him, like all the other riders, to talk about the future. Some went and were given salaries five times higher. I didn't get anything like that. I was at the end of my contract and I went to Molteni. I also realised that I was regaining my freedom. The tribal mentality got to me. The boss would order a beer and 11 guys would immediately order the same beer. The Tourmalet episode made me realise that I was only good for shining shoes and keeping my mouth shut. I had hoped for a little more recognition – that's what got to me, I suppose. But my decision to join Marino (Basso) at Molteni was the best one I ever made. Later that year, in a village in southern Italy, I met Antonia. She became my wife. Eddy and I never talked about that again. I have had so many other good times throughout my career.'

Even without the controversy that the Savona affair unleashed on the world of professional cycling, the summer of 1969 was unforgettable. Adamo, with his new song 'À Demain sur la Lune,'[8] in accordion-ballad style, couldn't have known how right he was. American astronaut Neil Armstrong was set to land on the moon aboard *Apollo 11* the day after the Tour's finish, on 20 July. It was a Sunday, and a joyful madness took over Brussels. A dozen trains, around a hundred coaches and thousands of cars made their way to Paris. It was the time when Brussels was dreaming of a successor to Sylvère Maes. 'It was the time when Brussels *brusselait*, a time when Brussels sang.' According

[8]'See you Tomorrow on the Moon'

to newspapers of the time, more than 10,000 people lined up in the La Cipale velodrome in Paris to celebrate Belgian National Day 24 hours early. '*La Brabançonne*' (the Belgian national anthem) rang out. Did Merckx himself even know that the lyrics were written by a Frenchman, Louis-Alexandre Déchet, and then modernised by another Frenchman, Charles Rogier? 'After centuries of slavery / The Belgian, arising from the tomb / Has reconquered through his courage / His name, his rights and his flag.' They could have been written just for him. At this memory Martin Van Den Bossche's face tightens, his jaw clenches to the point of cracking, emotion overwhelms him, and he stifles a sob. A second later it has gone.

We try our luck with one final question: 'How would you describe Merckx the champion?'

'Saying he was the best doesn't go far enough. He was a world champion, a universal champion. The word for him is still to be invented.'

'And Merckx the man?'

'I've said it all. We didn't always see eye to eye, but Merckx is a friend. You don't betray your friends.'

9 September, 1969: Merckx lies unconscious next to the velodrome track in Blois after falling during a Derny race

LA CIPALE, TWICE:
A TRAGEDY AND THE TOUR
DE FRANCE, 1970

'Being part of that inner circle required a discipline and rigour that permitted no let-up. We were compared to Caesar's Roman Legionnaires, which was the best compliment I'd ever heard.'

ITALO ZILIOLI, TEAMMATE

Perhaps we need a little break before we tackle the sixth professional season of the one who, aged 24, became a key figure in the peloton. The year 1969, which marked the start of a new era, was clear evidence of Eddy Merckx's progress on the roads of Flanders, Italy, Spain and France. The way he swept all competition before him during his first Tour de France was proof that there was a new phenomenon in cycling. His opponents were already riding in his shadow, and it wasn't long before they were only competing for second place. But it took almost nothing for his career to come to a screeching halt on the night of 9 September, 1969. It was on the cement track of the small velodrome in Blois, where he was competing alongside Jacques Anquetil, five-time winner of the Tour.

It was during a Derny race that tragedy occurred. The crew in front of him fell and Eddy's trainer, Fernand Wambst, was knocked off when he hit the small motorcycle that was left in the middle of the track. He was killed on the spot. Merckx fell heavily on his back 15m further on and hit his head on the cement border. The result for Merckx was a concussion and a dislocated pelvis. It was a lucky escape. His only protection was a rubber helmet with a little foam padding inside. The dislocation of the pelvis was more serious than it first seemed: 'After Blois, I could never quite find my usual pedalling rhythm in the mountains. I had less power in my left leg and a stabbing pain that forced me to keep changing position on the bike.'[9]

Yet the Merckx of the 1970s was there. And he was ready to go. Although he would have you believe that nothing would ever be the same again, the man from Brussels still looked to take on ever bigger challenges in 1970. After a Classics season where he won the Paris–Roubaix, Gent–Wevelgem, the Flèche Wallonne, the Belgian National Road Race Championships and the Giro – where he reaffirmed his supremacy – Merckx was ready for the next Tour de France. He was chasing a double that only Fausto Coppi (1949 and 1952) and Jacques Anquetil (1964) had managed before him.

In other words, nothing and no one could stop him. It was as if he was building on Machiavelli's fundamental principle, and that his first duty was to be strong and try to be stronger. Would anyone have thought him in any way diminished when he set off from Limoges on 27 June, 1970? His team was now Faemino, named after

[9] *Eddy Merckx: La Biographie* (Eddy Merckx: The Biography), 2015, Johny Vansevenant

a new instant coffee brand that had been launched by the Italian Carlo Valente, owner of Faema coffee. As with the previous incarnation, his teammates were all Belgian apart from Italo Zilioli, the Italian who replaced his fellow countryman Scandelli. It had become a Merckx constant: surrounded by teammates who had to be ruthless, ready to make any sacrifice for him and have no personal ego at all. But on the second stage, at the end of a 140km breakaway between La Rochelle and Angers, Zilioli won the sprint and relieved Eddy of the yellow jersey he had been wearing from the start. Was the boss angry? To find out, we had to go and ask the culprit who, strangely enough, was also his roommate for that Tour de France.

This quest led me to Ruffia, a small village of about 300 people in Piedmont, 50km east of Turin, which smells of lush grass and, when the bells ring, of livestock. What do you say about someone who gives you a hug instead of shaking your hand and then takes you into their confidence? 'Eddy and I hit it off straight away,' Zilioli starts. 'I witnessed and lived in the system during those years. All team leaders, as soon as the road started climbing, would grab on to a *gregario* [domestique]. Eddy, never. He was above the system. Everywhere, on all terrain. He was beyond categorisation. The day when Vincenzo Giacotto, the Italian manager of Faema, asked me if I was interested in being Merckx's *domestique*, I told him I would ride to Belgium on my bicycle if necessary to sign the contract. I only rode one season with them, and it was the most beautiful experience of my entire career. I never felt this emotion anywhere else. I rode well if I was happy inside, and friendship is happiness. You can't explain it. I remember everyone was happy to be there. The atmosphere was exhilarating. A friendship with someone is like a great love. You don't know why, it just happens to you.'

And who could disagree with such a man, who talks about cooking with such passion, who plays Edith Piaf songs on the accordion, who laughs all the time, loves cycling and is crystal clear about that famous stage of La Rochelle-Angers. 'You had to be in the breakaways to be in control, so I was up front. I got out of the saddle and I was off with a small group. On the flat, there were riders who were much bigger and stronger than me to shelter Eddy. Vandenberghe was there with me too. So we decided that the best way to make Eddy's rivals do the work was to set the pace ourselves. There was no controversy, despite what Driessens, our *directeur sportif*, came out with. Eddy's words were, in fact, kind: 'Don't worry, Italo. I'm not angry, just remember that a 140km breakaway takes a lot of effort – and the Tour is long.'

A few days later, on the cobblestones heading towards Valenciennes, the Italian, still in the yellow jersey, got a puncture. There's a rather striking image that shows Zilioli with a wheel in his hand waiting for the breakdown car that was taking its time. Meanwhile all the rest of the Faemino train rushed past him towards the finish, without a glance. 'I know there was a lot of talk about that picture. Puncture or not, normal service was resumed. The team had to be built around Merckx – I was just a footnote in the strategy. And if you think about it, the yellow jersey never left our room, from Limoges to Paris. In the evenings at dinner there was a good atmosphere. I sat next to Eddy, who translated Flemish for me. It was much more serious and sombre with Gimondi, who I rode with for several seasons. It was more tense, too. At the end of the meal, it was common for Eddy to tap his fingers on the table, imitating a tom-tom drum, and everyone would join in and do the same. It was the sound of war drums.'

Zilioli never complained. 'Being part of that inner circle required a discipline and rigour that permitted no let-up. We were compared to Caesar's Roman Legionnaires, which was the best compliment I'd ever heard.'

The man from Piedmont was all the more grateful to be chosen as roommate to the big boss, because he suffered from sleepwalking and could wake up screaming at any time of night. 'It did happen once during the 1970 Tour. I stood up on the bed, shouting, "Fire! There's a fire!" I opened the door and walked into the hallway. Eddy woke up, took me in his arms like a father would do with his *bambino*, and calmly put me back in bed. How could you not be exemplary out on the road after something like that? With energy from the heart, we can do great things.'

Between Limoges and Paris, the Belgian took the lion's share of prizes: eight stage wins, King of the Mountains, victories in the combined and combativity classifications.

'Daddy, just who is this Merckx that everyone is talking about?' asked Brigitte (aged eight) one day as she went to give her father a kiss. He was Christian Raymond, former teammate of Merckx – and a real character.

'He is a man who doesn't leave any crumbs behind for others to eat.'

'Then he must be a cannibal,' concluded the little girl.

Legends are even more beautiful when they come out of the mouths of children! Merckx made a career out of it. But in the climbs 'The Cannibal' was lacking his usual finesse – his pedal stroke just wasn't as fluid. Several times during the race he had to adjust his seat post to relieve his back. A shrewd observer was his former teammate who became an enemy, Martin Van Den Bossche. He didn't even need this small detail to know whether the yellow jersey was having a good day: 'I knew everything about him and I could tell right away when he was not on form. Before the start, when he was being overly friendly – shaking hands, stopping to chat – I knew he didn't have good legs that day. I could even tell from the way he combed his hair. So I would press him hard. Again and again. No one had done me any favours the year before.' Van Den Bossche didn't press hard enough to beat him to the top of Ventoux. Merckx climbed it for the first time while wearing a black armband as a tribute to Vincenzo Giacotto, who had died the day before. The long-distance match between the two Belgian riders ended after the arrival of the Tour's doctor, Dr Dumas, in an ambulance. Both riders were on the verge of fainting due to lack of oxygen and were placed under observation.

The old French guard – Poulidor, Aimar and Pingeon – had a disastrous Tour, as did Jan Janssen, while Gimondi had stayed at home. A generation of hungry young riders took the opportunity to make a name for themselves. No one knew much about Joop Zoetemelk, 24. He had won the 1969 Tour de l'Avenir but came in second in Paris on his very first Tour. A performance that the Dutchman relived six times in 16 attempts, before finally getting his hands on the Grail in 1980, aged 34. The emergence of young French riders was limited to a few stage victories, but the question was asked: Was one of them the man who could stand in the way of Eddy Merckx in the future?

The winners in question were: Cyrille Guimard (1st stage), Alain Vasseur (8th), Christian Raymond (19th), Bernard Thévenet (18th) and Jean-Pierre Danguillaume (22nd). Most significant was the young Thévenet. At 22, he was solid in the mountains and good against the clock, too. Gaston Plaud, Peugeot's *directeur sportif*, only let him know he would be riding three days before the start – almost as an afterthought. The rider from Burgundy knew he was carrying a few extra kilos and felt he was in 'very average' condition for a three-week race like the Tour. Some personal memories came flooding back. 'The very first time I saw Merckx – other than in a photo on the wall of our room at the Bataillon de Joinville – was in 1966 before a criterion near where I lived. I went to a restaurant with my parents. It was 2km from Guidon, the hamlet we lived in.'

There was another first time, this one on a bike, at the start of the Grand Prix de Monaco in 1970, at the beginning of the season, and another at the Mont Faron coastal time trial a month later. Thévenet could almost have framed this anecdote: 'Plaud made me go out first, but then a strong wind blew up and I had the best time right until the end. It was my first victory as a pro. Merckx himself had a problem at a level crossing and had fallen.' It is hard to picture what happened next, on the slopes of Tourmalet, on 14 July in the fog and rain. 'When I attacked at the foot of the Tourmalet, I was sure that no one thought I had a chance, because nobody moved. I have never suffered so much. It is so difficult to win a stage in the Tour that you never forget it when it does happen. When I got to La Mongie, I knew I was going to make a career of it and that I had earned my place in the peloton.'

Eddy Merckx praised Thévenet in the press the next day. Little did he know that five years later, the curly-haired guy with matching sideburns would be the one to stop him from claiming his sixth Tour de France title.

At the foot of the ascent of Mont Ventoux nicknamed the 'Bald Mountain', Ocaña (L), Merckx (C) and Poulidor (R) open the road during the 1972 Tour de France

Merckx wearing his world champion jersey and Faema cap, 1968

ORCIÈRES-MARSEILLE-MENTÉ: LA CIPALE, THIRD – TOUR DE FRANCE, 1971: THE PERFECT STORM

> 'I felt broken after 100k … we didn't even have time to ask for a drink. If we drifted even a little way, we risked being dropped.'
>
> ROBERT BOULOUX, PART OF THE ORCIÈRES–
> MARSEILLE STAGE BREAKAWAY

The Tour is a race for heroes. The 1971 edition, from Mulhouse to Paris, offers the perfect illustration of this. More than 50 years later it is always the same words that are used to describe it: drama, madness, recklessness. Because there is nearly always a blind, irrational element in a hero's behaviour; a kind of instinct that is stronger than they are, something they cannot escape. Let's get straight to it.

For this beautifully staged, three-act drama, history gave us two great adversaries.

In the blue corner: Eddy Merckx – already a two-time Tour winner, a world champion with a pile of Monument trophies to his name – surrounded by a team that operated like a crack military unit. In the red corner: Luis Ocaña, with the Vuelta a España in his list of honours. He only has one single stage victory in the Tour de France, but he has just won the Volta a Catalunya and the Tour of the Basque Country. He is definitely the most serious candidate to succeed Merckx. First and foremost, he was a relentless rival.

The 1971 Orcières–Marseille–Menté trilogy[10] is as much a Tour legend as Eugène Christophe's forks in Sainte-Marie-de-Campan or the Anquetil-Poulidor duel at the Puy de Dôme. The action, from the Hautes Alpes to the Pyrenees, passing through the Champsaur valley, is as romantic as the subject: the quest for the yellow jersey. And even when Joop Zoetemelk took the sacred jersey from Merckx in the 10th stage – won by Bernard Thévenet – it did not distract anyone's attention from the real battle: Merckx versus Ocaña. Since the Spaniard had won at Puy de Dôme, finishing 15 seconds ahead of the Belgian, and then pushed him 1 minute 36 seconds back two days later by capitalising on a puncture, the tension had ratcheted up a notch. Jean-Claude Genty, Ocaña's teammate at Bic and a front-row witness on the Tour, put it bluntly: "'That other prick" is what Luis sometimes called Merckx. He was certain that at last he was going to get the better of him. He had made his career out of the rivalry. It was both his obsession and his torment. He had to beat Merckx, but he feared him. Luis was a big character, and stubborn like you couldn't imagine. He was courageous, very Spanish, he

---

[10]This refers to Luis Ocaña's decisive attack at Orcières-Merlette and his subsequent crash on the Col de Menté, a dramatic turning point in the Tour de France.

had balls. And he never gave up. Perhaps just to convince himself more than anyone else, he would swear at the slightest opportunity – cross my heart and hope to die – "Goddamn it, I'm going to make that bloody Cannibal eat his bicycle."'

According to other accounts, he went as far as to name his dog Merckx, and had fun ordering him around: 'Merckx – sit. Merckx – give me your paw.'[11]

Listening to the protagonists of the time also means rediscovering two extraordinary people, two contrasting characters, two philosophies and two ways of looking at cycling. To describe them in five words, you'd say: perfectionism, work ethic, discipline, daring and courage for Merckx; fiery, generous, passionate, rebellious and tormented for Ocaña. There are those who say Ocaña would have won if he hadn't crashed, and those who claim Merckx would have closed the gap anyway, because the Spaniard was done. The two sides will never agree.

Before we go back to the first of the three important acts of the Tour – Grenoble and Orcières on 8 July, 1971 – it is important to note there was a change in Merckx. He had to always keep a spanner in his jersey pocket so he could adjust his seat post during the race, to calm his back pain. He knew that he wasn't going to get any better. The injury would cause him pain right up to the end of his career. Merckx packed a dozen pairs of shoes and a dozen bikes, and had his mechanic file down a pedal by just a few millimetres in order to achieve perfect symmetry.

And another observation, this time about their respective teammates. Without them, this epic duel would never have

---

[11]Johny Vansevenant, *Eddy Merckx: La biographie* (Racine, 2015).

reached such heights, and here we will name them all, out of respect (and for history):

Wearing the Molteni jersey – tan with a blue band – directed by Giorgio Albani: Joseph Bruyère, Jos Huysmans, Frans Mintjens, Jos Spruyt, Julien Stevens, Roger Swerts, Victor Van Schil, Herman Van Springel and Marinus Wagtmans.

Wearing the orange and white Bic jersey, with Maurice De Muer as *directeur sportif*: Roland Berland, Francis Ducreux, Jean-Claude Genty, Charly Grosskost, Bernard Labourdette, Désiré Letort, Leif Mortensen, Johny Schleck and Alain Vasseur.

Thursday 8 July, 11th stage, Grenoble–Orcières: the sky was bright blue. Eddy Merckx was not in a good mood. The previous day a puncture on the descent of the Col du Cucheron cost him his place with the race leaders. Lucien Van Impe, who ended the race as King of the Mountains, testified: 'When Ocaña realised that Merckx was no longer there, he said to us, "Let's go ride. This is our chance." On the Col de Porte, Merckx couldn't manage a comeback.'

But what bothered Merckx greatly was not just seeing Zoetemelk in the yellow jersey. It was 'the boos and the insulting gestures from the public on the Col de Porte', he confided to the Belgian journalist Louis Clicteur. Even in the Velodrome de Grenoble he was greeted by a concerto of whistles. France's anti-Merckx campaign was to continue for a long time and would only get worse. The Orcières stage – 134km long – was a minefield. The 18 per cent gradients of the Côte de Laffrey, where trucks from the local factory came to test their brakes, quickly exposed

Merckx's limitations. He knew he was going to have a bad day. His stomach pains started to resurface. He was in trouble, 'in agony', as he said himself. And there was no notable improvement further on, up the Col du Noyer.

Meanwhile at the front, Luis Ocaña was floating on his pedals, delivering the greatest performance of his career – one that he had announced that morning at the start. Roland Berland, one of his teammates, heard him say to the whole team: 'Right, today I'm going to bring him to his knees. Berland, Grosskost – you stretch the peloton to single file all the way to the base of the Côte de Laffrey. There, I'm going to attack – and settle the matter.'

'Be careful. An attack is good,' said Berland, 'but remember that from the top of Laffrey, it's still 100km to the finish line.'

'That's not your problem – it's mine,' replied Ocaña.

'It was serious,' continued Berland, 'and nothing like the way he sometimes did it in a more light-hearted tone when he'd call out to us, "Come on, you donkeys, let's go!"'

Jean-Claude Genty, who was astonished, adds, 'I'd never seen him like that before. Luis didn't know how to race tactically, but he had class, an animal instinct and immense pride. He drew immense strength from his resilience and his rebellion. That day he was better than Merckx.'

Throughout the 15km climb to Orcières, the peloton stayed on Merckx's wheel. He was alone, without a single teammate. Years later, he referred to that stage as a 'nightmare, I felt that the entire peloton had a score to settle and was trying to make me lose.'[12] To this day Genty retains

---

[12]Ibid.

an image he will never forget: 'The nobility of a defeated man, of great dignity. Even when he was suffering, Merckx maintained that lordly bearing. At one point, I found myself behind him, and I saw him crying. I promise you, he was crying, I didn't imagine it.'

Merckx paid a heavy price. He ended up 8 minutes and 42 seconds behind. Ocaña said that he finally had 'the wolf by the ears'. Who would have thought that the greatest heist in the history of the Tour would be set in motion the next day – the rest day in Orcières – before heading to Marseille? To simply state the facts is, inevitably, to open the door to passion and bias. Marinus Wagtmans was one of Merckx's teammates. Here's what he had to say about the swashbuckling atmosphere that prevailed. Wagtmans was the brains behind the operation to retake the lead, and provided considerable support for his leader. On a bike, 'Rini', as he is known, could do it all: ride, climb and especially descend. At team gatherings at the start of the season, he demonstrated that he could easily ride on the back wheel only for hundreds of metres. Pedalling a kilometre in reverse, or contorting himself and riding while passing his torso through the frame, were two of his other tricks. He was like a rubber man. On his insistence, Merckx and the Molteni team went to have a good look at the descent at Orcières, twice by bicycle, once by car. They noted that the first 20 bends were very tight, highly technical. The decision was made. As soon as the flag dropped, four of them would charge down the descent, which was about 15km long. The others would create a diversion around the yellow jersey so that he wouldn't suspect anything.

Saturday 10 July, 12th stage, Orcières–Marseille: swel-tering heat. In Tour director Jacques Goddet's editorial, he mentions a 'Saharan atmosphere'. Wagtmans, who now divides his time between the 'sunshine state' in the Miami area and his native North Brabant in the Netherlands, recounts: 'I had also involved other good descenders in the plan. Van der Vleuten, a friend, was warned, "If you want to come with us tomorrow bring a parachute." A few minutes before the start, I signalled to Ocaña, who was chatting at the back, leaning against the barriers with some journalists. He answered me with a wave of the hand. Merckx, Huysmans and Stevens were planted on the side. Mr Lévitan had not even finished lowering the flag when I had already gone 100m, Eddy right behind me.'

A ripple ran through the peloton – curses – everyone digs in and holds on. But it was too late. When Ocaña looked up, the leaders were already 500m lower down. Jean-Claude Genty confirms: 'There was no peloton, just riders scattered everywhere. The crashes delayed Luis, who also went down, though without serious injury. He must have fallen three times in the first hour. It took another hour before a proper chase could be organised.'

At the front, Robert Bouloux, who wasn't afraid of anything on a descent, had the right reflex: 'When I saw Wagtmans I jumped to it, but he was already two bends ahead. Even at the bottom, I was still 50m behind. It took me a kilometre to close the gap. Then during the sprint, Merckx, Huysmans and Wagtmans yelled at each other in Flemish to encourage one another. They were the only ones riding. I felt broken after 100km. There was a heatwave, and we didn't even have time to ask for a drink. If we drifted even a little way, we risked being dropped.'

There is a very thin line between madness and recklessness. But, with eight minutes to catch up, risking the impossible was all they could do. At the Old Port, the lead of the nine breakaway riders – Aimar, Armani, Bouloux, Letort, Paolini, Van der Vleuten and the three Molteni riders – was only 1 minute and 56 seconds. But the speed! They were averaging more than 46km/h and were an hour and a half ahead of the best time. They hadn't even finished putting up the crowd barriers and Gaston Defferre, the mayor of Marseille who was supposed to hand over the yellow jersey, was still sitting on the plane that had just landed at the airport.

It wasn't looking good for Merckx. It didn't matter. As Hamlet put it, 'To fight even for a scrap of straw when honour is at stake has always been the mark of heroic souls.' And Eddy Merckx has that nature.

Luis Ocaña is another heroic soul, you can't take that quality away from him. After the finish, Wagtmans continued to spy on the yellow jersey rider. 'He had been helped by a good portion of the peloton in the chase, but I wanted to see his physical condition. I was astonished to see that two people had to support him to get to the podium, and he needed help to get up the steps. At that point I knew it wasn't over. He had used up far more energy in that chase than he realised. I knew Ocaña well, he would always act proud. But after that he wasn't quite the same.'

Monday 12 July, 14th stage, Revel–Luchon: a thunderstorm was forecast. Before arriving in Luchon, 214km further on, there were climbs up the Portet-d'Aspet, Menté and the Portillon. The Molteni team plan hinged on the recovery of Luis Ocaña, still in the yellow jersey. The Spaniard hoped that strategic alliances could save his jersey. The group riding for Luis towards Marseille included Zoetemelk's Flandria team and Guimard's Mercier team, 'to whom Ocaña had promised the green jersey if they collaborated', adds Wagtmans.

As a result, Merckx and his group no longer had a choice. They had to go on the offensive and go all out on the climbs. On the early slopes of the Col de Menté, that shrewd 'Rini' Wagtmans could see that with each burst of acceleration, Ocaña dropped back 10 to 20 metres and took a little longer to catch up each time. He also noticed large white stains beneath the armpits of the yellow jersey. 'He had lost a lot of minerals. There was no way he could keep up that pace for 200km.'

On the road to Menté the mercury was already nearing 30°C. The thunder that had been rumbling in the distance was much closer. Thunderstorms? They'd cycled through them before, although they'd never cycled through a tempest like the one about to break right over their heads. It was wild and brutal. Robert Bouloux remembers what it was like on that road to hell: 'After one minute there was a flood, water and hail. The road was a wild torrent, full of mud, branches and hailstones. As I tell it, I feel like I'm back there.'

A memory from Bernard Thévenet: 'We were almost at the top and the sky was black, it was like night. The wind whipped up and the storm immediately followed.

A crashing, violent storm. The road just disappeared. It was one of the most dangerous moments of my entire career. One of the few times I was afraid.'

Merckx had already crested the hill with a 20m lead over Ocaña, and he was charging ahead. 'We had no brakes,' says Joop Zoetemelk. 'You had to use your feet to stay upright, but with the mud streams we were sliding all over the place, the bikes were out of control. At the bottom of the descent my shoes were in tatters, they looked like slippers.'

And then: drama. On an almost impossible hairpin bend, Merckx fell. He scraped his knee on a rock but got up immediately. Ocaña was not so lucky; he fell off in the same place. As he got back up he noticed a few broken spokes on his front wheel. But he didn't see Zoetemelk, who was off balance and aquaplaning down the wet road, hurtling straight towards him. There was a violent impact. Agostinho also hit the yellow jersey rider, who was lying on the ground writhing in pain.

Thévenet again: 'I saw the yellow jersey on the ground, and if a mechanic hadn't stopped me I would have gone into him too. In the evening during his massage he replayed the events. Why did Ocaña take such a risk? Later, I learned that the Spanish side of the race was passing through a small village where his parents once lived. Pride and vanity can take you a long way. But you can't change people's character – they are no longer the same – and if he hadn't carried that pride within him he might not have attacked the way he did in the Orcières stage.'

The next day, *L'Équipe* featured the unforgettable head-line '*Le Tour Foudroyé*' ('Lightning Strikes Tour'), and in his column, Antoine Blondin praised Luis Ocaña's struggle, with the magnificent phrase: 'When the sun went down twice.' More than 50 years later, Jean-Claude Genty, the faithful teammate, has not changed his story: 'His hubris did for him. He should never have tried to follow Merckx. At times he could be very awkward on the descent, so I still carry this doubt: even if he hadn't fallen, I still don't think he would have beaten Merckx.'

In the Molteni camp, there is no doubt; there is conviction. 'Luis always had an off day in a Grand Tour. He was completely spent and about to crack. That fall gave him an honourable way out,'[13] says Wagtmans. As for José Manuel Fuente, winner in Luchon after finishing outside the time limit in Marseille, then reinstated amid controversy – along with the entire Kas team – he was annoyed to see that no one was paying attention to him. 'You're going to regret this,' the Asturian rider had threatened. 'Tomorrow, I'm going to make the whole peloton finish outside the time limit.'

There were five stages left until La Cipale – enough for the Molteni team to settle the score with those who had ganged up against Merckx. The big loser was Cyrille Guimard, to whom Ocaña had promised the green jersey – The Cannibal made it a point of honour to take it himself. A crosswind attack between Mont-de-Marsan and Bordeaux, with the help of his teammates Roger Swerts and Julien Stevens, settled the matter.

Later, ironically, Merckx said of Guimard: 'His jersey must be stuck in a pine tree somewhere in the Landes.' This voracious attitude earned The Cannibal even more

---

[13] *Les Hommes de Merckx* (Merckx's Men), 2007, Patrick Cornillie and Johny Vansevenant

criticism, but Jacques Goddet, on the contrary, welcomed it: 'That's what racing is about – the pursuit of victory, not small concessions made to keep the crowd happy.'

The nearly three-time Tour winner also knew that you had to spare the competition sometimes. Jean-Pierre Danguillaume, Bernard Thévenet's future road captain, would take advantage of that during the 18th stage, between Bordeaux and Poitiers. 'After the Aquitaine Bridge, Eddy approached me. "Hey – you've got a light wheel on the back with a 180-gram tyre – you're up to something. Sorry, but one of my teammates will be on your tail."' In Ruffec, 70km from the finish, the rider from Tours was firmly in the breakaway, but, as promised, he had Jos Spruyt right behind him.

Danguillaume said, 'The finish was on a tartan track, and I knew that to win, I absolutely had to be at the front. I needed that win. My wife had told me that we only had 54 francs (£7) in our bank account and we owed 4,000 francs (£534) to the builder. I asked several guys in the breakaway if they were willing to do the last kilometre for me, and I got nos from all of them. There was only one left, Spruyt, and I said to him, "Joseph, will you ride for me?" Without saying a word, he did the job and I won. That evening we were in the same hotel as the Molteni team and I asked Merckx how much I owed for the helping hand. "That's between the two of you," he told me. I gave some cash to Spruyt, who added, while he shook my hand, "Next time it'll be a lot more expensive."'

Yellow jersey, green jersey, combined classification, four stage wins: for his first season with Molteni, Merckx more than fulfilled his side of the contract.

That year, deep in the Côtes d'Armor in Brittany, a teenager has just discovered a passion for cycling. He is from Yffiniac. To earn some money, he works at a petrol station on the weekends. Soon he earns enough to buy a Gitane bike from his brother Gilbert. On a spring Sunday in Planguenoual, he takes part in his first race. The next day, the newspaper *Ouest-France* devotes a quarter-page to Bernard Hinault's first victory.

Merckx (C) on the podium with Poulidor (L) and López Carril (R)
on 21 July, 1974 in Paris after winning his fifth Tour de France

LA CIPALE, FOURTH: TOUR DE FRANCE, 1972

'Luis was the man for spring and the Tour. Eddy
was the man for all four seasons. The best thing
was that he was in every race to win it, not just
for training like some of the riders you see today.'
ROLAND BERLAND, DOUBLE CHAMPION OF FRANCE,
OCAÑA'S TEAMMATE

In winning the 1972 Tour and earning his fourth consecutive victory (1969, 1970, 1971, 1972), Eddy Merckx equalled
the feat of Jacques Anquetil (1961, 1962, 1963 and 1964).
The man from Normandy had won a fifth (1957), the man
from Brussels hadn't – yet. The return of the Merckx-
Ocaña duel – cut short in 1971 after the challenger was
forced to abandon the race in the Pyrenees in the 14th
stage – ended with the same result in 1972. Taken ill, Ocaña
did not even contest stage 15.

That year's Tour, which ran from Angers to Paris, and
in which no Spanish teams took part, was notable for the
awful weather. There were thunderstorms, high winds
and temperatures that struggled to get over 13°C. It was
everything that the Spanish champion disliked. And his

bronchitis became a lung infection. After abandoning the race, Ocaña did not resurface until the end of the season. And although he was second in the overall ranking for three days – in Merckx's shadow – Roland Berland, Ocaña's former road captain at Bic, says: 'I never felt he could win that Tour. He wasn't right. He was dominated from start to finish. It was the opposite of 1971, where I had witnessed the great – the really great – Ocaña. He would say, "Merk, Merk, Merk (that's how he pronounced it), what does he have that I don't? I'll get him. I will bring him down."' It is when he was angry, when the blood was boiling in his veins, that the Spaniard from Mont-de-Marsan showed how he was truly a great champion: the Ocaña from Orcières in 1971, his crowning moment. 'He would often lose his temper over "that savage who attacks all the time",' continues Berland.

Merckx was his greatest rival, and knew his temperament. The Belgian was ever provocative and would deliberately try to get at him. 'Which only made Luis even more furious,' recalls Berland. 'There weren't many who dared to challenge him like that, in public.' The former two-time French champion of that era (1972 and 1979) raises another issue – Ocaña's personality, which quite likely got in the way of achieving the greatest goal of his career. 'Luis was a man of extremes. He could go from euphoria one day into worry or despair the next – and when you have such a monumental obstacle blocking your path, it gets really difficult. But there is one thing you can never take away from him, and that's the enormous energy he put in to beating Merckx. Luis was a man who was capable of extraordinary feats. And in Orcières, he was like the great Merckx himself.'

In this playground game for grown-ups, they were playing 'who's the strongest?' Ocaña had a shortcoming that
Merckx didn't: his health. 'Ocaña was more fragile, he
needed sunshine,' recalls Berland. 'Luis was the man for
spring and the Tour. Eddy was the man for all seasons. The
best thing was that he was in every race to win it, not just
for training like some of the riders you see today.' Their
pride would never again clash with the same violence as it
did on the 1971 Tour. Merckx skipped the 1973 Tour, and
Ocaña, after his win that year, withdrew from the 1974
Tour with a fractured elbow.

But let's go back to 1972. Before he showed up as the
big favourite on 1 July in Angers, Merckx had not been
idle. In addition to victory in his third Giro, he had won
two Monuments: Milan–San Remo and Liège–Bastogne–
Liège. He added a third at the end of the season, the Tour
of Lombardia. And as if he needed to set himself a new
challenge, he went to Mexico on 25 October to break the
hour record (49.431km/h). He ended up with 50 wins in
127 race days: simply monstrous. It was like the Twelve Tasks
of Hercules on a bicycle; nobody has ever bettered him.

In 1972, Merckx was in his eighth season and had never
let up since his professional debut in 1965. Everybody knew
that his strength manifested itself best in long, sustained efforts.
And that after a season on the road, he would already be
preparing for the winter: Six-Day races, from Gent to Berlin,
Maastricht to Grenoble, Antwerp to Milan. But there was
another explanation: it could be genetic. The Belgian journalist Rik Van Puymbroeck lives in Meensel-Kiezegem, in
Flemish Brabant, 20km from Leuven, the same village where
the young Eduard Louis Joseph Merckx was born on 17 June,

1945 (a Sunday, just before dinner), in a house with red brick walls, on Tieltsestraat. There are still members of the Merckx family there. It was through one of their distant cousins, Rémi Roskins, that the journalist from *Bahamontes* magazine gained access to this information: 'Eddy's maternal grandfather, one Theophiel Pittomvils, had herculean strength. He could lift a 100kg bag of grain with one hand and load it on to a trailer. Would it not be unreasonable to conclude, given all the power and resistance that Merckx developed over the seasons – with more than 150 race days on the road, winter nights in velodromes where he would win, always win – that he inherited something from those genes?'

When the peloton entered the Pyrenees and started up the Aubisque, it was Guimard, not Merckx, in the yellow jersey. Ocaña was already nearly three minutes behind at that stage. Racing in the rain and cold, the wearer of the Spanish champion's jersey fell off on the descent from the Col du Soulor. In the crash, he took Alain Santy and Bernard Thévenet with him. The former was evacuated by helicopter. The latter, who hit his head against a low wall, had a scalp wound and no longer even knew which race he was in.

'It was awful,' recalls Thévenet. 'I was up and ready to go again, like a robot. I didn't pass out, but I did lose part of my memory. Up until February, I could remember everything, my memory was fine, but after that – nothing. Instinctively, I turned to the Peugeot team car. I could see the Tour de France sticker stuck on the windscreen and I remember thinking, "Why on earth has Gaston gone out with a car from the Tour?" So I asked him: "Are we in the Tour de France?" "Yes," he replied. "Seriously, Gaston. Where are we, which race?" At the same time, I dug into the pocket of my jersey and pulled out the stage map with the profile. I saw that we had to climb the Aubisque, which in fact was already behind us. I finished as best I could, in tears and still in a daze. Dr Brossard, who stitched me up, told me it was a concussion. And I was thinking, "Just as well we didn't go up the Aubisque – that would have been really tricky."'

After a night in observation at the hospital, the man from Burgundy was out the next day. '"You shouldn't really leave," the doctor said. "If you feel your head spinning, stop right away." But that's how I saved my '72 Tour. I had two stage wins after that – Mont Ventoux and the Ballon d'Alsace.'

When racing, Merckx ignores all sentimentality. Former journalist Joël Godaert once asked him about his irrepressible need to rack up victories. The reply: 'Christmas is for giving, not a cycling race.'

The Belgian champion was about to win his fourth Tour de France and his second Giro–Tour double, joining Fausto Coppi, whom he would surpass two years later by winning the Giro d'Italia and the Tour de France again for a historic triple, which has never been equalled since. While he has frequently been depicted as 'a tireless, insatiable, obsessive, enraged rider'[14], it would be more accurate to say that Merckx harboured a wild, devouring passion for cycling that totally consumed him and instinctively led him to extraordinary feats, including Mourenx, Marseille, Tre Cime di Lavaredo and Mexico City. You could add Mendrisio, Liège, Roubaix, San Remo ... the list is too long.

He was in yellow from the 18th stage, and it seemed like a done deal. But not quite, because Eddy also wanted

[14]*Dictionnaire Amoureux de la Belgique* (Dictionary for Lovers of Belgium), 2015, Baronian

the green jersey – for the points ranking – which was still worn by Guimard in the 18th stage. It was no secret that the two men did not like each other. The situation had been made worse when Guimard had appeared to openly collude with Ocaña the previous year between Orcières and Marseille. Merckx did not like conspirators. There were three stages left for him to earn the 40 points that separated him from the green jersey.

As it turned out, he only needed one. Guimard, who had had a very good Tour – four stage wins, yellow jersey for seven days, did well in the mountains where he beat Merckx in the sprint at Revard – was forced to abandon the race between Pontarlier and Auxerre, his knees gone. On the podium, the quadruple winner of the Tour de France was flanked by two old riders: Felice Gimondi, 30 (1965 winner), who finished second, and Raymond Poulidor, 36, third, who earned his sixth podium finish. (He ended up with eight at the end of his career.)

But there was a surprise waiting for the Belgian champion after his lap of honour at La Cipale. Félix Lévitan, the director of the Tour, approached and pointed out Guimard, who had come to the finish in civilian clothes. Merckx himself continues: 'Mr Lévitan asked me if I would be willing to give my green jersey to Guimard. I was a little surprised, but I did as he asked. There was no sympathy on my part – I mean it. That gesture, captured in photos, where I handed the green jersey to Guimard, went completely against the grain for me. It was all an act. And then in that jersey – that I won – he did all the post-Tour criteriums.[15]

---

[15] *Eddy Merckx: La Biographie* (Eddy Merckx: The Biography), 2015, Johny Vansevenant

Some time earlier, the final of the Premier Pas Dunlop (the ancestor of the Junior French National Road Race Championships) took place in Arras, Pas-de-Calais. The all-new champion of Brittany takes part. He breaks away from the peloton and rides solo for the remaining 60km to the finish, where he wins with a handful of seconds to spare. The next day in *La Voix du Nord*, Jean-Marie Leblanc, journalist and future director of the Tour de France, devotes a front-page headline to the winner: Bernard Hinault.

23 July, 1972, Paris: Eddy (C) celebrates his fourth Tour de France victory but hands the green jersey to Cyrille Guimard (R)

6 July, 1970: Merckx during the 10th stage Belfort–Divonne-Les-Bains of the Tour de France, followed by his team's manager Guillaume Driessens

LA CIPALE, LAST: FIFTH TOUR DE FRANCE VICTORY, 1974

'I had to fight so much, battle for this yellow jersey, make so many sacrifices…'

EDDY MERCKX, FIVE-TIME TOUR WINNER

Questions were being asked in the late spring of 1974: Is he on the decline? Is this the end? Is there a health issue? From 1966 onwards, Eddy Merckx had always won at least one Monument to launch his season: Milan–San Remo, Tour of Flanders, Paris–Roubaix, Liège–Bastogne–Liège were all on the list, with the Tour of Lombardy as the finale. That year he could manage no better than fourth in the Tour of Flanders and the Paris–Roubaix, and the low but telling whispers of his fading dominance were starting to circulate. The reasons given by The Cannibal were 'bronchitis' and 'relapse'. It was enough to keep him out of the Milan–San Remo and Ardennes Classics. By way of a more in-depth explanation, the main man added for the pessimists: 'It'll come, don't worry.'

The rest of his schedule was a long way from that of a rider in recovery. For the first time, Eddy Merckx tackled the Giro d'Italia, the Tour de Suisse and the Tour de France consecutively – and won all three. At the Giro, Merckx came up against the great José Manuel Fuente, known as 'El Tarangu' ('the fiery one' in Asturian), a nickname passed down from father to son. Regarding him, Merckx always said that he was 'an unpredictable climber, the one I feared the most because of the aggression of his attack.'

In this Giro d'Italia, the rampant leader of the Spanish Kas team – who wore the pink jersey for 11 days, won five stages and was King of the Mountains – pushed his provocation to the point of tying a handkerchief to his right sleeve to indicate that he was on the warpath and would not yield. 'Even we had a hard time dealing with it at times,' said Gonzalo Aja, his teammate from Santander who was also his friend, and a famous climber too. 'He did only as he pleased and trusted no one and nothing except his legs. He relied solely on his instincts.'

When we arrived at his house Aja was about to go for a ride on the roads of Cantabria. His ritual has lasted for half a century. Five times a week he enjoys two hours of free- dom in the mountains and on the small, wild coastal roads. 'My head asks for it, my body needs it – it works for me.' And in that famous year, 1974, he, too, was one of Merckx's challengers on the mountain roads of Italy, Switzerland and France. 'El Tarangu had got it into his head that he would win this very mountainous Giro. And not just win it – he wanted to see Merckx on his knees. "I'm going to put him a quarter of an hour behind." It was his obsession. I have never seen him as strong as he was in that Giro. He was better than Merckx and everyone. He nearly made it, we did too. The day before the last big stage in the Dolomites, he got us all together in his room to tell us how it would happen. He would attack from the start and those of us in the peloton would protect him by sticking to Merckx. We had already done the sums and allocated the money. There was enough for each of us to buy an apartment. Fuente attacked as he said he would, but 20km from the finish, he suddenly stopped dead on the road. He was utterly drained, and our winnings evaporated. We had to push him to the end of the stage. Merckx had already been there for a quarter of an hour.'

It was during this Giro that Merckx learned of the death of Jean Van Buggenhout, his long-term manager – and the only person who he allowed to say, 'I'm telling you what you should do, not what you want to do.' This bad news had greatly affected him, just as he had been equally touched in 1970 by the loss of Vincenzo Giacotto, a key figure in the Belgian champion's career. Without Giacotto he would never have had his 'Italian campaign' – from Faema to Molteni – nine astonishing racing seasons. Merckx said the following about Van Buggenhout: 'He was not a father figure or a friend who you confide in whenever you had a problem. Jean was a kind of guide who dealt with everything: contracts, money, teammates. All we had to do was pedal. After he died I had to do everything.'

The Tour de Suisse was more comfortable, with a victory and three stage wins. At the same time, the man from Brussels received confirmation that the Kas team, even without Fuente, was a formidable racing machine. Miguel María Lasa, Vicente López Carril, José Antonio González Linares, Gonzalo Aja and Txomin Perurena were relentless riders, strong on all terrains and always ready to go into battle. They more than proved it on the road during the 1974 Tour: López Carril (3rd), Aja (5th), Perurena was the best climber and Kas also won the final team classification.

In Switzerland, tacit agreement was reached between Eddy Merckx – aiming for overall victory – and the Spaniards, who were chasing stage wins and prize money, the interests of one aligning with the economic goals of the other, and vice versa. No one had forgotten the Giro experience – 'a disaster for the wallet!' joked Aja. Thanks to the mountains in Switzerland, the climbers on the Kas team had a chance to bounce back – and that's exactly what they did. 'You don't get anything for free,' continued the rider from Santander. 'No one gifted me the uphill time trial at the start of the Tour, nor the queen stage in Bellinzona. I recall that the winner received a one-kilo chocolate ingot as well as a real gold ingot. Merckx wanted to buy it from us, but there was no way. To avoid trouble with customs, we deposited it in the safe of a French bank. It was worth half a million pesetas. The following year, gold took a tumble and the ingot was worth only half as much. We shared what was left.'

Merckx seemed to have regained his morale as well as his health before heading for Brest, the starting city of the 1974 Tour. The abscess in the saddle area that had been bothering him in Switzerland had been lanced. The doctors assured him that the scar was healing well. How could he not be calm? The fates had conspired to clear his path to victory: Ocaña (elbow fracture), Zoetemelk (skull fracture), Van Impe (wrist fracture) were absent and Thévenet was severely weakened by a bout of shingles he contracted on the Vuelta a España. His number one rival was Raymond

Merckx wearing the yellow jersey between Mulhouse and
Strasbourg during the 2nd stage of the 1971 Tour de France

Poulidor, 38 years old but still a threat. Was Merckx's fifth success in five attempts (he didn't even take part in 1973) his easiest, or just the least complicated? You might think so, given how much he dominated: 20 days in the yellow jersey and eight stage victories. Raymond Poulidor had indeed got the better of him in the mountains – at the Pla d'Adet – but five days from Paris, Merckx's lead over the Frenchman was still six minutes, and the Tour became his playground. Five yellow jerseys, three green jerseys and 32 stage wins – a total he increased to 34 the very next year. That stage record stood for half a century until Englishman Mark Cavendish – the formidable sprinter from the mid-2000s, winner of Milan–San Remo 2009 and the World Road Race Championship 2011 – claimed a 35th in 2024. In a sprint – of course – and just like all the others, after 15 entries. Cavendish had a second coronation at the age of 39 when he was made Knight Commander of the Order of the British Empire in 2024.

But let's pedal back to that glorious month of July 1974. When questioned about his total domination, this feeling of owning the Tour, Merckx remained measured, and tempered the enthusiasm of Théo Mathy, his compatriot: 'I had to fight so much, battle for this yellow jersey, make so many sacrifices...' The press interpreted this as a form of respect for his opponents.

But the reality was quite different. On the 1974 Tour, Merckx nearly lost everything. In Switzerland, on several occasions he was seen taking his famous spanner out of his pocket and adjusting his seat post. He was still suffering from pain in the legs and back, the distant but stubborn consequences of his fall in Blois in 1969.

Eddy adjusting his bike to mitigate pain during the Tour de Suisse 1974

Without realising it, he had been over-compensating and had taken up a bad position. The resulting wound had become ulcerous and had to be treated. A scalpel cut – however small – only a week before the start of the Tour de France is never insignificant. What none of Eddy's rivals would ever know during those three weeks from Brittany to Paris, passing through England, was that the wound had reopened. It was bleeding enough for his shorts to be sodden by the end of each stage. The loyal, lamented Jos Huysmans, a team-mate from the very beginning, was very clear: 'The weather was nice and dry, thankfully. If Eddy had had to ride half the Tour in the rain, I think his wound would have become infected and...' Every night Eddy had to take a sitz[16] bath, alongside anti-inflammatories to relieve the pain.

[16] A warm, shallow bath for soaking the hips and buttocks to relieve pain, itching and swelling in the perineal area between the genitals and anus

Another, slightly more obscure event – possibly even unknown until now – became part of the history of the 1974 Tour. Gonzalo Aja, second in the general classification from the 11th stage onward, was the surprise package. In Salève, Ventoux and Galibier he really showed what he could do. He even sat up on some of the other climbs to let his great friend, the much-missed Perurena, take the lead. Everyone on the Tour was wondering, 'who is he, what's he doing, what's he up to?'

By the time they left the Alps, Aja was right behind Merckx. In five days' time the peloton would reach the Pyrenees. The Spaniard was sure of it: 'That's where the Tour will be decided. That's where I'm going to win it.' And then one morning, just after he woke up, he saw that someone had slipped a note under his bedroom door. It is forever etched in his memory: "If you carry on, you'll be in big trouble. Go home." For a few days I had two policemen in the corridor of my hotel at night. Then we arrived at the great Pyrenean stage. I had been waiting for it since the start. Five mountain passes: Canto, Bonaigua, Portillon, Peyresourde and Pla d'Adet. I circled them in red on my book. I ignored the threat. I was calm. When I woke up, I felt great. We had hardly gone 5km from the start at Seo de Urgel when an Italian rider slammed into me violently from the side. I hit the rocky wall and fell hard on my backside. The X-ray revealed a sacral fissure, and the Tour turned into a nightmare. "If you fall on it again," the doctor told me, "you'll do permanent damage." What do you do? Do you stay or go home? I had nights with only three, four hours of sleep because of the pain, but I still finished fifth in Paris.'

When Merckx said he had 'seriously suffered and seen all sorts in the mountains,' he knew what he was talking about. And his dramatic gesture on the slopes of Saint-Lary-Soulan, where he threw his bike and grabbed another, spoke volumes. Wounded in the body and jostled in the mountains, surely the fatal blow was not far away.

A popular saying states that the Tour de France is for the 'Giants of the Road'. Tom Simpson (the first Briton to wear the yellow jersey, Tour de France 1962), Barry Hoban, Brian Robinson, Graham Jones, Paul Sherwen, Robert Millar, Mickael Wright, Sean Yates, David Millar, Chris Boardman, Maximilian Sciandri, Adam and Simon Yates, and especially Sir Bradley Wiggins (winner of the 2009 Tour), Christopher Froome (four-time winner in 2013, 2015, 2016, 2017), Geraint Thomas (victorious in 2018), Sir Mark Cavendish (record holder for stage wins, 35), Luke Rowe, a strong opponent of doping, Fred Wright, Ben Turner, Sean Flynn and Tom Pidcock all belong to this dynasty of the 'Giants of the Road'.

It is equally important to include Irish riders in this prestigious list. Seamus Elliott, Stephen Roche (winner of the 1987 Tour), Sean Kelly, Martin Earley, Paul Kimmage, Dan Martin, Sam Bennett and Ben Healy, the latest revelation of the 2025 Tour, also deserve this honourable distinction.

Other nationals from English-speaking countries have seen in the Tour de France – its legend, its media coverage (images reach as far as China), and its millions – a new Eldorado. In a pendulum effect, this time the gold seekers heading for the Old Continent are Americans. Although Donald Allan was the first Australian to pin on a race number in the 1974 Tour, in the US, Jonathan Boyer is considered a pioneer (1982 Tour).

But it was with Greg LeMond, best young rider of the 1984 Tour, that the New World became excited and got swept up in the frenzy. Rightly so – LeMond was both an exceptional rider and a miracle survivor. The winner of the Tour in 1986, he suffered a terrible hunting accident the following year. Having lost 60 per cent of his blood, he survived and went on to win two more Tours de France (1989 and 1990).

Following in his footsteps came a pack of young wolves dreaming only of conquest. Andrew Hampsten, Alexi Grewal, Eric Heiden (five-time Olympic gold medallist in speed skating at Lake Placid in 1980), Ron Kiefel, Davis Phinney and Jeff Pierce became 'Giants of the Road'. And since everything is done bigger in America, multinationals like Motorola Inc., Discovery Channel (owned by Warner), and the United States Postal Service (the government postal service) unlocked colossal budgets. Every means was employed to chase the yellow jersey, and the Tour de France, born in 1903, entered one of the darkest periods of its long history.

This was the beginning of the Lance Armstrong era – seven-time winner between 1999 and 2005 – later stripped of all titles for blatant violations of anti-doping regulations. A symbol of an America angry at someone who once had an open invitation to the White House, *Sports Illustrated* awarded him the title of 'Most Unsportsmanlike Athlete of the Year' in 2012. Frankie Andreu, George Hincapie, Tyler Hamilton, Kevin Livingston, Floyd Landis, Levi Leipheimer, David Zabriskie, Christian Vande Velde and Bobby Julich were all caught up in this unprecedented scandal. Lesser-known riders like Jonathan Vaughters,

Chris Horner, Tejay Van Garderen, and Andrew Talansky contributed to restoring the image of the American cyclist – a legacy that Sepp Kuss, Neilson Powless, Matteo Jorgenson, Brandon McNulty and Quinn Simmons strive to uphold.

Donald Allan, the first 'Aussie', set the example. Phil Anderson, Allan Peiper, Stephen Hodge, Neil Stephens, followed by Henk Vogels, Robbie McEwen, Stuart O'Grady, Bradley McGee, among others, were worthy successors. Then came Cadel Evans' victory in 2006, rewarding a continent's passion. Richie Porte (3rd in the 2020 Tour), Adam Hansen, Simon Clarke, Caleb Ewan, Rohan Dennis, Michael Matthews, Jay McCarthy, Ben O'Connor, Jai Hindley, Jack Haig and Jay Vine have successfully bridged the gap to the 'New Wave', now carried by Callum Scotson, Michael Storer, Kaden Groves, Luke Durbridge, Chris Harper, Chris Hamilton, Michael Matthews and Luke Plapp – far from the untouchable Tadej Pogačar, but Giants nonetheless.

Let's backpedal and return to the 1974 Tour. Jean-Luc Molinéris, on his first Tour de France in 1974, who won a stage but was forced to abandon the race with illness in the 20th, is also a Giant. For three weeks, the young man from Cannes was wide-eyed. His father was Pierre Molinéris, a native of Caraglio in Piedmont, a friend of Coppi and the winner of a stage in the 1952 Tour riding for the Sud-Est team. At the start of Jean-Luc's career, Pierre sent him to experience the cobbles and crosswinds alongside Maertens, Demeyer, Godefroot, Pollentier and Dierickx at Flandria. There was no better way to learn how to jostle in the pack and earn respect. The sixth stage of the 1974 Tour finished in Harelbeke, Belgium, a real *flahute* (Flemish 'super tough guy') stronghold.

In the final stretch, he saw Merckx himself shutting down every move from those trying to catch Ludo Delcroix, one of his own, and Michel Pollentier, who had broken away. 'When Merckx decided, no one could get out of the peloton,' says Molinéris. 'It was clear that he wanted to favour Delcroix, his teammate. But with 20km left I thought, "it's now or never", so I went for it. Just as I stood up on my pedals, Merckx turned his head, saw me and was about to follow, when he settled back down. Did he think I wouldn't be able to catch Delcroix and Pollentier? I'd rather think that he liked me and gave me a chance. I'll never forget that gesture of his. Later I was on his team. But I never asked him about it, I'd rather write my own end to the story – it's nicer.'

Eddy Merckx had joined Jacques Anquetil in the Pantheon of five-time winners of the Tour. What was going through his mind during his last lap of honour at La Cipale – the last time it would host the Tour? A sixth victory? That was not out of the question. This way he had of starting one thing while already thinking of the next – as if his future depended on it – is one of the fundamentals of Merckxism. To feel that time doesn't stop – to chase it, even outrun it. After all, up until then he'd always been right. Why change a winning formula? Because of his failed Spring Classics campaign? On 25 August, 1974, on the Mount Royal Circuit in Montreal, Merckx became world champion for the third time. He was ahead of Raymond Poulidor, who came second, just as on the Tour. Everything was in place for a sixth Tour victory.

Not far away, 20-year-old Bernard Hinault has just become French pursuit champion – using wheels borrowed from Daniel Morelon, the multiple world and Olympic sprint champion. In the Route de France race, the Bretton triumphs in the major mountain stage. On the podium he is warmly congratulated by Louison Bobet. For him, too, a new chapter is about to start.

Merckx (C) with Jacques Anquetil (R) and Felice Gimondi (L) in August 1969 before the start of the criterium

*Merckx (L) puts on his raincoat with the help of his faithful
teammate Jos Huymans at the Züri-Metzgete Classic, 1975*

PRA-LOUP:
TOUR DE FRANCE, 1975

'To be a great champion, you have to go over the Izoard Pass in the yellow jersey. You're already halfway there.'

LOUISON BOBET, THREE-TIME WINNER OF THE
TOUR DE FRANCE (1953, 1954, 1955)

Eddy Merckx did not win a sixth Tour de France. The 1975 Tour, which was very mountainous – five peaks – settled the question for that year. That July, the entire cycling world was captivated. Luis Ocaña, Joop Zoetemelk, Bernard Thévenet, Lucien Van Impe and – of course – Eddy Merckx would make the Tour exhilarating, emotional, fascinating and tragic. The five-time Tour winner set off in his 11th professional season, hardly concerned about his age. He was 30 years old, and still traversing the globe like one of the great explorers of yesteryear. He had 150 race days in 1974, and as many again by the end of the next year. He didn't want to see the wheel of fate turning. The idea didn't even occur to him. In the spring, he got his biggest ever haul of Classics: Wins on the Milan–San Remo, Tour of Flanders, Liège–Bastogne–Liège and the

Amstel Gold Race, as well as two placings: Paris–Roubaix (2nd) and the Flèche Wallonne (3rd). His unshakeable energy and his never-ending desire led him to the foot of the summit: he wanted a sixth Tour de France, maybe even a seventh.

The truth was that after such a successful Classics campaign he had chosen to compete in the Giro d'Italia and to skip the Tour de France. He wasn't feeling particularly enthusiastic about its tricky route. But a sore throat, a bronchial infection and a fever meant he had to give up the Giro two days before it set off from Milan. The Tour became a priority. Merckx prepared for the Tour by racing the Tour de Romandie (14th), the Critérium du Dauphiné (10th), and the Tour de Suisse (2nd), where he was given a rude awakening: in the big mountain stage of the Dauphiné, Thévenet gained an 11-minute lead over him. The remaining 20 days were not enough for Merckx to bridge the gap.

In Charleroi, at the start of the 1975 Tour, the young Italian Francesco Moser (first time in the Tour but hardly a débutante – he had won Paris–Tours and came second in the 1974 Paris–Roubaix) beat him in the prologue, taking the yellow jersey by just two seconds. Everyone knows what happened next. Twenty-one days later, Bernard Thévenet paraded in yellow down the Champs Elysées – the first to overcome The Cannibal. For the whole of France – waiting for that moment since 1967 when Roger Pingeon was the winner – saw it as the good guy beating the bad guy. They couldn't take any more of the seemingly insatiable Merckx, who gobbled up everything in front of him. Over the years, the nation had gradually come to detest him – until it went too far, and some idiot did the undoable on the climb up to the Puy de Dôme. 'I was spat at, stones and insults were hurled at me, I was booed, and there was the assault. At that point I realised I was in danger and that the whole country did not want me to win.'[17] After Merckx's defeat in Paris, the journalist Robert Janssens recounted this astonishing sentiment: 'Once I had lost, they applauded me and encouraged me as if, suddenly, everything was fine and I was one of them.'

When a Tour de France plays out like that one, on the border of fact and fiction, with dirty tricks, the rumours that spread get out of control and take over from reality. And so it was that the alliances forged along the way by Maurice De Muer – the man who transformed the Peugeot team – were, for the Merckx camp at least, what made Thévenet's victory possible. In addition, the violent kidney punch given by that idiotic spectator on the climb to the Puy de Dôme *was* (not *would have been*) the cause of his breakdown on the climb to Pra-Loup.

Regarding this latter rumour, you could certainly argue that in the terrible Col d'Allos a few kilometres earlier, the Belgian champion was crushing everyone, and felt nothing. As for the first rumour – regarding a so-called 'friendly little handshake' or two – they are as old as the Tour itself. When Moser admitted in *La Gazzetta dello Sport* that he had, on a few occasions, sided with the Peugeot team, it was mainly to make clear to Merckx that he didn't think much of him. 'I ride where it's in my best interests. They

---

[17] *Eddy Merckx: La Biographie* (Eddy Merckx: The Biography), 2015, Johny Vansevenant

(Peugeot) made the effort to talk to Filotex. I never saw anyone from Molteni reach out.'

The truth about the race is altogether more rational: Thévenet's legs went faster than Merckx's. The Frenchman proved it on the Izoard – and there it had nothing to do with circumstances or alliances. His greatest advantage was undoubtedly having beside him a *directeur sportif* who was as crafty as a fox, a true leader – and a great strategist capable of outwitting anyone. As Thévenet himself said: 'Without Maurice De Muer, I'm not certain I would have had the courage to take those risks, especially at just the right time.' The Tour would not be the Tour if it didn't have drama.

They say that the player deserted by luck always draws the bad card, and after that setback at Puy de Dôme came Valloire. The peloton had not yet left the neutral zone. It was riding along at 10km/h when the most unbelievable, unlikely crash occurred, sending Eddy Merckx tumbling to the ground. A move by Ritter was the cause. The toll was heavy: a double fracture of the upper left jawbone and a fractured sinus. There were six days to go, but there was no question of him abandoning the race: 'It was my way of paying tribute to the dedication of my teammates who had worked so hard to try and help me win. What's more, if I had left the Tour they would have lost a lot of money since I was still in second place; it would have felt like a betrayal.'

It was on the climb up to Pra-Loup in the Alpes de Hautes Provence that the classification of the 1975 Tour was reversed with perfect symmetry. In Puy de Dôme on the evening of the 14th stage, Eddy Merckx was still in the yellow jersey, ahead of Bernard Thévenet by 58

seconds. At the end of the 15th stage, Pra-Loup, the difference between the two men was still 58 seconds – but now
it was the other way around: Thévenet was in first place
with the yellow jersey, Merckx was 58 seconds behind,
in second place. What remains of those magical moments
on the road to Pra-Loup for the man from Burgundy?
Of that first podium in a yellow jersey, of the ascent of
the Izoard the next day: what does he remember 50 years
down the line?

It's a February morning in the Café de la Gare, Grenoble.
It's before the lunchtime rush, and I am face to face with
Bernard Thévenet, my recorder ready to go. We've only
been talking for five minutes, and it's like he's already
put his white Peugeot jersey back on, the one with the
chequered pattern, bib number 51. You can tell he's keen
to get going on that 15th stage. It's a climb of five mountain passes: La Colmiane, Couillole, Les Champs, Allos and
Pra-Loup. He goes over the passes with his fingers, a lump
in his throat. I listen silently. He tells the story. The 1975
Tour winner has a glint in his eye:

'I must admit from the start that ever since the Dauphiné
when I had beaten him, I no longer saw Merckx as some
otherworldly figure. I saw him as just another rider. Just
one of us. According to De Muer's plan, I could be no
more than 2 minutes and 30 seconds behind at the foot of
the Pyrenees. Job done: Merckx was wearing the yellow
jersey and I was 2 minutes behind. In Fleurance on the first
rest day, Merckx had told journalists: "My most dangerous
opponent is Thévenet." And when Merckx put a target on
your back you knew it was no joke. He noticed everything about his rivals: thin tyres, gear setup, lightweight

wheels – nothing escaped him. Even the smallest error could cost minutes. There were leaks of our battle plan. I had planned to launch an attack on the Col d'Allos, but it all went wrong. I was held up by a puncture on the descent of the Col de Couillole. My teammate Raymond Delisle helped me bridge the gap, but I had used up a lot of strength in the pursuit and I couldn't attack on the way up to the Col d'Allos. Merckx could tell straight away that I hadn't recovered, and it was he who went on the attack 800m from the summit. I have seen photos of Eddy's descent from the Col d'Allos – it is simply amazing, unreal – it was pure madness. The Bianchi car fell down a ravine. Motorcyclists had told it to slow down, but Eddy was going even faster. At that same time, I had a hypoglycaemic episode. My legs went to jelly. I had nothing in the tank. I simply couldn't keep up. I ate something. My legs still felt soft. At the foot of Pra-Loup I must have been 1 minute 10 seconds behind, and I was angry.

'I closed the gap on Van Impe and Zoetemelk, then left them behind. My energy returned. I heard spectators shouting about the narrowing gap, and I started to believe that I could catch him before the summit. And suddenly I rounded a corner and there, before my very eyes, I saw the Molteni car in front of me. At first I thought it was a trick to make me slow down, but no, Eddy was there, slumped on his bike. I can still see a patch of melted tarmac, right in the middle of a bend. Eddy took the corner on the inside, while I hugged the left, steering clear of the melted tarmac and, crucially, making sure he wouldn't be able to get on to my wheel. I couldn't believe he could be caught out like that. He was never caught out.

'I kept on pushing. I knew that Gimondi was still in front. I caught up with him 1km from the end. That last kilometre was one of the hardest of my entire life. In the end, we were all at our limit, all on an equal footing. It came down to courage. I crossed the line and fell off my bike. I could hardly breathe. I didn't even hear the announcement that I had won the yellow jersey. Our mechanic, Jean-Claude Vincent, told me. Straight away, I said, "Oh shit. That means tomorrow we'll have to hold on to it." And then we were on the podium; Eddy and I both wearing a yellow jersey. It was funny. It was total chaos on the podium. The press were there, people were shouting, flashbulbs were popping. I didn't know where to stand, I nearly fell off a few times. You can just see it: "New yellow jersey winner snaps his clavicle falling off the podium." Eddy congratulated me and he meant it, I'm sure. We've got to know each other since then; I can even say that we understand and appreciate each other. But I also knew that with him it was never over, and that I would have to dig deep the next day.

'On the first night, as I said in the Preface, I went to the bathroom in the middle of the night. I could see the yellow jersey on the back of a chair, lit up by the moon. I said, "Hang on, why did Eddy leave his yellow jersey in my room?" It took a long time for me to come to terms with it, to be able to stay in control under all that pressure. One evening a journalist from *France-Soir* came to my room at ten o'clock at night; I let him in.

'The next day was a short stage. The Tour would be won or lost on Izoard. I have never seen so many people on the way to the Casse Déserte. It was a human sea with just a narrow way through in the middle of the road. If I hadn't had a motorbike guard with me I would never have been able to make it. I still meet people who say to me: "We were there, it was amazing, magical. Thank you." It was so thrilling, I nearly pushed myself into the red. At the finish, Merckx was more than three minutes behind me. The next day on the starting line, Louison Bobet came over and shook me by the hand. Louison had been one of my first heroes. I was inspired by reading and re-reading his book, *En Selle* (In The Saddle). And then he looked me in the eye, and he said this: "To be a great champion, you have to go over the Izoard Pass wearing the yellow jersey. You're already halfway there."

'The 1975 Tour changed my life. People no longer looked at me as "Nanard" – my nickname – now I was a Tour winner and the man who had knocked Merckx off his perch. When I look back at that first week I realise I learned a good lesson. Eighty per cent of supporters' signs were for Poulidor, 20 per cent for all the others. For many people, we did not even exist. When I won the yellow jersey, everything changed. Poulidor pointed it out to me one day on a stage: "You know, from now on, it's not just about you." After that experience, I always thought that the glory doesn't belong to you alone any more. It belongs to your supporters. They are the ones that make you look like a great champion or not.'

Bernard Thévenet had done it, and Bernard Hinault was not far away. On 1 January, 1975 the young man from Brittany signed his first professional contract with Gitane-Campagnolo under the direction of Jean Stablinski. His teammates included Lucien Van Impe, the best climber of the 1975 Tour de France and the first-ever wearer of the polka-dot jersey, future winner of the 1976 Tour Maurice Le Guilloux, and Georges Talbourdet. Hinault's first meeting with Eddy Merckx took place in the Paris–Nice. Then came Milan–San Remo and the Dauphiné: 'And then,' he exclaimed, 'it turned out that Merckx had two arms and two legs, just like everyone else.' 'The Badger' was born.

*In the Pyrenees, Merckx entrusts his tireless teammate Jos Huysmans
with the task of setting the pace during the 1972 Tour de France*

ALPE D'HUEZ:
19 JULY, 1977 – THE LAST
TOUR DE FRANCE

'Bernard Hinault will be the best rider in the world.'
EDDY MERCKX, INTO THE MICROPHONE
OF JEAN-PAUL BROUCHON (FRANCE INTER),
SAN CRISTOBAL, VENEZUELA

The destiny of this timeless champion demanded that he get back in the saddle quickly – Merckx was convinced he wasn't defeated on his true merit in the 1975 Tour de France. He had fought a lost battle, not perished at his Waterloo as some proclaimed. For Eddy Merckx, the goal was unwavering: rise above the hyperbole and win a sixth Tour.

Summer is green and blue. It is criterium season, just as we would say strawberry season. The masses lap it up. It is worth taking a moment to discuss criteriums, because they were so intimately linked to cycling culture before they all disappeared, one by one. The criterion was a major social event at the time. In 1970 in Caen, the first of the year attracted a crowd of more than 100,000 spectators. In the mid-1970s, there were about 100 in France and double that in Belgium, where they were called *kermesses*. Cycling contracts are still very modestly paid.

In Belgium, Merckx gets 70,000 Belgian francs (around £1531) just to start a race. A decade later, following his 1986 Tour de France win, the American Greg LeMond raced in the Netherlands for 500,000 French francs (£67,250). In 1976, Robert Mintkiewicz, as a teammate of yellow jersey winner Lucien Van Impe, earned his place as a special guest. 'I accompanied Lucien everywhere in France after his victory in the Tour. I wasn't getting much, only around 2500 francs (£353), but multiply that by 41 criteriums, and that's not bad.'

From north to south, east to west, they meandered around the main roads in their powerful cars, moving from a *ducasse*[18] to a funfair, from one local celebration to another. In the middle of the afternoon or in the evening, under the plane trees – on *la promenade* or down a shaded boulevard (Victor-Hugo, for example) the drum majorettes paraded, the brass band played and the riders, in colourful silk jerseys, were the stars of the show. On the colourful posters, bold letters announced the billing of a yellow jersey, of the Tour's best climber, of a green jersey. Thévenet. Merckx. Van Impe. Godefroot. Ocaña. Zoetemelk. Guimard… And, almost bigger than the cycling stars themselves, the name of the announcer, the master of ceremonies, the man who would transport the crowd to a land of wonders, even sing songs by famous French singer Charles Aznavour to them. The likes of Mario Cotti, Jean Tamain, Jean Gillet and Maurice Jouault were the first *As du micro* ('aces of the mics').

---

[18] Annual local festival in villages and towns in Belgium and northern France

One fine day during the golden age of criteriums, a remarkable figure bursts on to the scene – an outsider full of talent. He has expertise, wit and tenderness. The young Daniel Mangeas (commentator on all the Tours, and hundreds of other cycle races, from 1974 to 2014) is 25 years old. He comes from Saint-Martin-de-Landelles in Normandy, where there's a church with a road going around it. There has been no one like him since.

Generally, the magic of a late summer's evening ends around two hours later. People don't seem to really care whether the results of these 'chipolata criteriums' – where the riders parade by like sausages in links – were maybe a little bit pre-arranged. The grown-ups come along and would remember them until the winter, the little ones would dream of them until next year – or maybe forever. Sometimes, nothing goes to plan.

It was the night of 7 August, 1970 in Saint-Cyprien, a seaside resort near Perpignan in the south of France. Eddy Merckx was supposed to win, but on that day Luis Ocaña's vanity caused him to race his own race. He attacked from the start and spectators witnessed a frantic duel between the Belgian and the Spaniard, which lapped the peloton over and over again as if the other riders did not even exist.

There was another moment of brilliance – stars brought down to earth – in a criterium in Belgium. Ocaña tried to play it cool at the start, saying, 'Hey guys, let's take it easy today.' Merckx paid no attention. Attacking right from the off, Merckx blew straight through the peloton. With Ocaña hanging on his back wheel the duo soon lapped the field once. Twice. Three times.

Other stories breathe life into a picturesque era – one that has gone for good. After his win in Bussières in the Loire in 1970, Eddy Merckx stopped in the suburbs of Valencia. The following day, the hotel owner immortalised that historic night, putting up a picture frame: 'Eddy Merckx, the great cycling champion, slept here at the Logis des Oliviers, in room 12, on 24 August, 1970.' Another time, in 1975, the five-time winner of the Tour visited Callac on 29 July. The double jaw fracture he suffered in Valloire a few days before meant he still had to eat the children's menu: minced beef, mash and fruit compote. The following evening he was set to perform under the lights at a track meet in Le Blanc, Indre. Jean-Pierre Danguillaume, a close friend and fellow rider from their days racing in Callac, offered him a place to stay in Joué-lès-Tours. Arriving late at night, Merckx asked his host, 'What time do you get up?' Danguillaume responded, 'Between 9 a.m. and 10 a.m. – why?' Merckx replied, 'Nope, we're up at 8 a.m. and doing 50km on your training route.'

That morning ride – side by side with Merckx through the scenic Joué-lès-Tours countryside, from the Grottes Pétrifiantes in Savonnières to the Gardens in Villandry – left Danguillaume with an unforgettable memory. 'Around halfway, we stopped for a pee. There was an apple tree by the road and we each picked an apple, sat down on the grass and ate it in silence in the sunshine, as we listened to the birds singing. But that evening in Le Blanc there were no gifts: Merckx, first, Danguillaume second.' In France, throughout his career, Merckx must have won at roughly 30 criteriums, and 10 times more than that in Belgium. He turned up at the start of a criterium as casually as Jean-Paul

Belmondo, a prolific French actor, walked on to a film set: a mere formality.

A perfect storm of pride and confidence had swept through France in the wake of Bernard Thévenet's win in 1975. But trouble was brewing right from the start of the following year. The outgoing winner was forced, through sickness, to abandon the Tour in the 19th stage. That left the field free for Lucien Van Impe to cross the line in Paris as winner on his eighth attempt. As for Eddy Merckx, although the seasons – 1976 was his 12th – had taken their toll, nothing could take away the nobility with which he tackled the final quests of his career.

The best illustration of this is probably his seventh victory in the Milan–San Remo. The worn-down Belgian champion was plagued by health issues throughout the 1976 season. He suffered from sinusitis, saddle sores and lumbago – not to mention a nasty injury to the elbow which meant he could only grip his handlebars with one hand on the cobbled parts of the Brabantse Pijl. He blamed his poor results in the Tour of Flanders, Paris–Roubaix and Liège–Bastogne–Liège – where he was never even one of the frontrunners – on the antibiotics he was taking. During the Giro d'Italia, his abscess became infected. It required an operation. He was ruled out of the Tour de France and would have to wait another year before attempting to get his revenge and a sixth victory. His lumbago was triggered while he bent down to pick up a pear. He admitted, 'I had to lie on a wooden board for six weeks – I couldn't even make it to the bathroom. To get around I had to crawl with my hands.' His end-of-season record was the lowest of his entire career: 15 wins from 111 race days.

But the worst was yet to come. The financial situation of his Italian sponsor had deteriorated sharply. Alarm bells had been ringing for the team under Ambrogio Molteni and sons since 1974, in the form of late – even missed – payments. Merckx bailed out his teammates with his own money. Over the course of 1976 he had to pay for his own medical care, including the hospital. The Salami King was eventually convicted for fraud, black market dealings and other shady schemes. He was fined 1 billion lire (£458,540) and Merckx would never recover the back pay he was owed, some 52 million lire (£23,810).

After nine seasons in Italy riding for Faema, Faemino and Molteni, Eddy Merckx returned to France in 1977. His chosen team was Fiat France, where he would be working under Raphaël Géminiani and Bob Lelangue – his former teammate and confidante. Two French riders formed part of the adventure: Robert Bouloux and Jean-Luc Molinéris. The other 12 riders were Belgian or Dutch. Molinéris recalls, with genuine pride, 'While Géminiani took care of the journalists and Lelangue looked after logistics, Merckx made the decisions. He was absolutely the boss, but the heavy responsibilities that weighed on his shoulders had no influence whatsoever on the atmosphere within the group.' At the very start of Molinéris' career, during a race in Catalan Cycling Week, 'Merckx made his team ride so fast that it actually made me want to give up cycling. I felt totally and completely out of my depth. Strange to think that five years later I'd be wearing the same shirt as those "motorbikes" Sercu, Bruyère, Huysmans, Swerts and Schoenmaecker. Eddy was no longer the fiery rider of the great Merckx years but he still commanded respect. I can still see it. He had such presence – the way he could give an order with just a glance, and the way he kept those secrets that concerned the whole team. No one knew that during the 1977 Tour he had been battling mononucleosis (glandular fever). My holy grail was when I was chosen by Sercu to be his lead-out man in the sprints. Patrick knew that I didn't like the jostling, and he said, "Go flat out until the last 500m. I'll take care of it after that." He bagged three stage wins on the 1977 Tour, and I was dead chuffed to have played even a small part.'

Robert Bouloux's signing nearly fell through. As he says himself: 'I had come in third in the 1976 Tours–Versailles, so I asked Géminiani if he could do a bit better than the paltry amount he was offering. The next day in *L'Equipe*, without even talking to me about it, Gem announced that I had been sacked. It talked about "Bouloux's demands" in the paper. They said it was my fault we'd lost Tours–Versailles to Poulidor. The day after that I was out of a job. But I didn't back down; I walked through the door to Mr Lévitan's office and told him what had actually happened at the Tours–Versailles finish – he knew nothing about it. There were three of us on the break: De Witte, Poulidor and me. I suggested a partnership to Raymond but he turned me down. Everyone knew how mean Poulidor was when it came to spending money. De Witte, on the other hand, was up for it. "I'm in," he told me. So I led him out for the sprint, which he won easily.

'"So, where do you want to ride next season?" asked Lévitan. "With Merckx," I replied. "I'll take care of it. No problem. Go home, don't worry." I was reinstated but I was still on that tiny salary.'

No particular memories from that season with Merckx resurface, apart from a dressing-down from Géminiani. Bouloux, again: 'In the 1977 Tour, Gem really caused a fuss. He seemed to have it in for me – I've no idea why. During one stage where I was in a breakaway with Zoetemelk, Van Impe, Ocaña and others – without taking a single relay – he came over and tore into me, saying my place was back next to Merckx, not out front trying to look good. I was shy, I didn't go and apologise to Eddy that evening. I felt crushed just thinking about his win record. Images of the great Merckx sometimes come back to me. In the Liège–Bastogne–Liège where he attacked a hundred metres after the start, on the first climb. Unbelievable! The entire peloton was in single file with Merckx all alone out front, 400m ahead. At the top of the climb there was a bit of crosswind. He turned around to look and the first riders caught up with him. Immediately, an echelon formed. He only needed 5km to trap and wear down the other favourites. I'll say it again, and I really mean it, during that '77 Tour, I worked like crazy. In the team time trial that we won, I was right on Bruyère's wheel, and when I took the relay I can tell you that behind us the elastic was being stretched. The boss must have been happy with me for him to suggest that I follow him to [team] Wilkinson, but it fell through and I gave up cycling at the age of 31.'

It was in Avoriaz at the end of a coastal time trial that Bernard Thévenet took the yellow jersey. German rider Dietrich Thurau – quite the revelation and also leader for the first 15 days – held on for two more stages, but he collapsed on the climb up the Alpe d'Huez. It was a similar

story with Merckx, who was second in the general classification until the 15th stage. He was ill and endured an
ordeal on the climb to the top of the Alpe. He finished 13
minutes and 51 seconds behind Hennie Kuiper, who came
in first. This latest hammer blow did not prevent him from
reaching Paris and giving journalist Robert Janssens the
scoop on an unbelievable piece of news: 'I'll be back next
year – to win.'

In the meantime, he was just an observing bystander in
the Thévenet-Kuiper duel, with the two separated only
by a gap of eight seconds before the time trial in Dijon.
It would be an exaggeration to claim that Merckx actually wanted the Frenchman to win a second time, but
through two gestures he demonstrated the high esteem
he held for Thévenet. The Frenchman says: 'In Dijon, as
he had started a good 15 minutes before I had, instead
of returning to his hotel, Eddy waited by the road, 3km
from the finish, a stopwatch in his hand. When I went
past, he shouted, "22 seconds ahead of Kuiper!" That gave
me the strength to finish. Eddy didn't have to do it. He
must have been feeling broken inside, but he waited for
me. Top class.'

The second gesture took place on the Champs Elysées,
before the departure of the 6km time trial in the penultimate stage. Thévenet again: 'At Peugeot, our bikes were
equipped by a French supplier, Maillard, who specialised
in freewheels, hubs and pedals. For this last time trial, I
had a back cog with 13 teeth on it. But I had heard that
Campagnolo had brought out a new one with 12 teeth.
I asked my mate Eddy, who told me: "Yes, it's true. We've
been using it in our team for three weeks. If you want, I'll

lend you a wheel with a 12-tooth cog." I did my time trial with a 56 x 12 gear and – for the record – I beat Eddy by three seconds.'

Merckx had just lost his second Tour de France. Weakened by mononucleosis, Merckx could do no better than sixth and his destiny began to resemble a parable: that of the vanquished champion who, driven by his inner strength, transforms into the anti-hero. In 1977, Adamo, Merckx's famous compatriot, sang a famous song about choosing your own path, with lyrics that reflected Merckx's career downturn. In the States, Bob Dylan was still singing 'The Times they are a-Changin'. They were indeed changing and the eternal nature of generations dictates that one wave will submerge another. The new wave of cyclists included Bernard Hinault, Francesco Moser, Freddy Maertens, Jan Raas, Marc Demeyer, Eric Vanderaerden, Sean Kelly and Adrie van der Poel, and they were already making their presence felt. He didn't really understand it himself, but The Cannibal harboured a certain sympathy for the man everyone called 'The Badger'. Eddy was in the front row to witness Hinault's wins in the Gent–Wevelgem and Liège–Bastogne–Liège in 1977. And he sacrificed himself and dedicated much effort to help the Frenchman win the Dauphiné that same year. Even better, following the UCI Road World Championships in San Cristobal, Venezuela, Merckx said the following into the microphone of Jean-Paul Brouchon of France Inter: 'Bernard Hinault will be the best rider in the world.'

At the end of 1977, for the first time, Eddy Merckx no longer looked young.

*On the climb of the Col de Menté, Merckx (in the lead) accelerates, ahead of
Ocaña, Van Impe, and Thévenet during the 1971 Tour de France 1971.
A few kilometers later, the descent will prove fatal for Ocaña*

Merckx during his last race, the 1977 Tour de France

ITALY, LOVE AND BETRAYAL: ADMIRATION AND CORRUPTION

'Eddy was more afraid of me than he was of Gimondi. He never knew when I was going to attack. Sometimes I didn't even know myself. I was always coming up with new things, like Leonardo da Vinci.'

GIANNI MOTTA, WINNER
OF THE 1966 GIRO D'ITALIA

In 1968 Eddy Merckx decided to pursue his career in Italy. His new sponsor was Faema. They were number one in the coffee machine market and wanted to boost exports to Belgium. The founder, Carlo Valente, had been running the team since the end of the 1950s with Rik Van Looy in it, and he wanted another prestigious name to succeed the Emperor of Herentals. Vincenzo Giacotto, the experienced, cunning manager (who exuded Italian elegance), suggested the young Merckx, who at 22 years old had two Milan–San Remos and a rainbow jersey on his CV. 'He has all the skills and all the talent,' he told the boss of the coffee machine empire. Enough to succeed Van Looy? The manager from Piedmont was a passionate admirer of the champion from Brussels and knew he was built for the sprint, but little more. Giacotto had a good reputation in cycling. The arrival of Carpano – a vermouth distiller – into cycling sponsorship at the end of the 1950s was down to him. Fausto Coppi (who never drank a drop) and Ferdi Kubler, the winner of the Tour de France in 1950, agreed to come and see out their careers there. Following them was a parade of riders who wore the team's black and white striped jersey (similar to the Juventus football team): Gastone Nencini (1960 Tour de France winner), Nino Defilippis (double champion of Italy, 1960 and 1962), Franco Balmamion (Giro winner 1962 and 1963) and Italo Zilioli (two-time runner-up in the Giro, 1964 and 1965).

Before the 1967 Flèche Wallonne, a test camp was organised in Cervinia, Val d'Aoste. Merckx had to climb the mountain pass, which is 2000m high, 15km long and has gradients that hit 12 per cent, under the supervision of Nino Defilippis, a former cycling star from Piedmont who offered to follow the young Belgian in the team car. At the top, his verdict was immediate. According to the book *Mes Champions* by the Italian journalist Beppe Conti, he said: 'I took Giacotto to one side and I told him, "Get him to sign a contract right now. On a scrap of paper if you have to. For life if he wants – and give him whatever money he wants, no arguments. That man can win everything."' The Italian manager never made a mistake in his professional choices. But he would barely have time to appreciate the many qualities, talents and daring feats of his champion. His tobacco addiction caused his death in 1970 at the age of 47. In the late summer of 1967, on the eve of the UCI Road World Championships in Heerlen – which he won in the sprint ahead of Jan Janssen and Ramon Saez – Merckx signed a three-year contract with Faema. His annual salary of 1.2 million francs (£161,038) was triple what he was earning at Peugeot, where he no longer saw eye to eye with Gaston Plaud, the *directeur sportif.*

The Belgian champion was happy in Italy, finally leading a team he had chosen. 'I will strike the soil of Italy, and legions will emerge,' Julius Caesar said before his attempt to conquer the world. Fascinating, even for a conqueror on a bicycle. Merckx would almost forget that he was in the country of Machiavelli. Between 1968 (his debut) and 1976 (his final season), the name Eddy Merckx gained a power and aura that harked back to the times of legend. '*Merckx come Coppi*' (Merckx like Coppi) headlined *La Gazzetta dello Sport* on the front page after his stunning performance at the Tre Cime di Lavaredo in the 1968 Giro. 'He changed the course of cycling history,' declared the Italian daily. His exploits were often measured against those of the *Campionissimo* – the saint of saints, the ultimate benchmark in the eyes of Italians.

At the end of his career, wearing the Fiat France jersey during the 1977 season, at a pre-season training camp, Merckx, whose list of achievements far surpassed Coppi's, was annoyed by this dwelling on phantom memories; of the fixed ideas that the most fervent embraced like Ulysses hugging his mast. Addressing Raphaël Géminiani, he asked: 'Everyone talks about Coppi, but what does he have that I don't?' 'Gem', a contemporary of the *Campionissimo*, didn't hold back in his reply: 'To start with, he won two races you'll never win – two individual pursuit road World Championships. In 1947 he beat Bevilacqua, another Italian, and in 1949 he dominated Gillen from Luxembourg. And, finally, he was 20 years ahead of the game. He revolutionised diets, invented interval training and was the first to wear a jersey with pockets on the back for better aerodynamics, and which the rider could fill with provisions. And he was the first rider to wear a silk shirt on a racetrack.'

No need to dig deeper to fuel my desire to go back to the source. I had been to breathe the air in Flanders, but in order to meet the people who made Belgium a cycling El Dorado in the 1970s, it was necessary to go on a pilgrimage to the land of Alfredo Binda, Fausto Coppi and Gino Bartali. For it was on these roads that Merckx first showcased the thousand and one facets of his immense talent. His legacy was five Giros, seven Milan–San Remos and two Tours of Lombardy.

The Milanese suburb of Rozzano, Tuesday 6 February 2023: the sky is pink with the late afternoon light. Amid the mingled scents of espresso and pastries in a typical bar-gelateria on Via Buozzi, Marino Vigna, 1960 Olympic team pursuit champion in Rome, is deeply moved as he recalls his memories. He transitioned seamlessly from the end of his racing career at 29 years old to the *directeur sportif* role at Faema in 1968, where he was younger than many of his own riders. From his first days with the young Merckx, Marino Vigna has forgotten nothing – not a single detail. 'This happened in Reggio Calabria, at the beginning of the season, during a training camp. One morning Vittorio Adorni, who was the leader for the Italian races and probably a little ill at ease from Merckx's temperament and confidence, sidled up to me and said, "We must show them who's boss, make it clear for everyone." So, "Vitto" mapped out the route for the training ride the next day. It was very tough, to challenge Merckx. He was crafty and had brought two other riders into the plan, Casalini and Armani, I think. It was under race conditions – no one had time to talk – and towards the end on the climb up Santa Elia, which was 15km long and very steep, things got heated. We were half-way down when Adorni came up to my car: "You'd better call it a day, or Merckx is going to leave us all behind."' And in an almost solemn tone, Vigna emphasizes each word as he continues: 'There was no arrogance in Merckx's gestures or his words, just complete confidence and conviction. He had respect for everyone. He was well-mannered, likeable. But once on a bike he was unrecognisable; it was the law of the jungle. At age 22, he demonstrated exceptional maturity. Adorni was already 30 and had won a Giro. He had the ambition, but he was no longer up to the task.'

Merckx ahead of Motta in the Milan–San Remo final in 1967.
They will finish in that order on the Via Roma

For his first race of the 1968 season, Merckx was entered in the Trofeo Laigueglia in Liguria, Savona. The cream of the professional peloton was in the starting line-up. The very lively race suddenly hit an unexpected obstacle: a closed railway crossing with a freight train stopped in the middle of the tracks. Vigna recounts: 'The riders went over the barrier and scrambled over the carriages to get to the other side and continue. There was about 20km left, and there was all to play for. Merckx, in the world champion jersey, wanted to do the same, but the stationmaster, assisted by a few *tifosi*, stopped him. We had to get Mario Milesi, our mechanic, to slip under the train with the bicycle while Merckx got past the others and picked it up the other side. But it was too late. Dancelli had taken too much of a lead. I don't know if I ever saw Eddy that upset ever again.'

Giacotto was pretty sharp, and when he recruited Adorni it was to have him help out as an advisor during and after the race as well. One of his key tasks was to change the eating habits of his young teammate. Vigna explained: 'In Belgium, they had a very different diet from ours. On the morning of a stage we had chicken liver and ravioli on the menu. In Italy, on the first three days of a stage race it was like the diet of someone who was ill: white rice, steak or ham. You didn't overload the liver; you avoided making the body expend extra energy on digestion. Leave the table hungry was the rule. When he arrived, Eddy weighed 76kg. Three months later he had dropped to 72kg.'

Adorni proved to be an astute nutritionist. He confiscated the biscuits, chocolate, gingerbread and cans of fruit in syrup that lay hidden at the bottom of suitcases. Vigna laughs out loud as he recalls: 'Guido Reybrouck and a few others would get together to secretly eat bread soaked in sweet wine. In the end, everyone was on board with the dietary discipline.'

The 1968 Giro was decided on the climb up the Tre Cime di Lavaredo, the symbol of the Dolomites. Austria is on the other side. The setting – three giant menhirs at a 2400m altitude – was where George Lucas later came to film scenes for *Star Wars*. There was a touch of science fiction in the 12th stage, Gorizia–Lavaredo, contested under horrific weather conditions that almost went beyond human endurance. Rain, hail, snowstorms – the 12km of the climb are forever etched in the memory of those who were there. Martin Van Den Bossche, Merckx's best team-mate in the mountains: 'It was so cold that the bike chain kept freezing. The mechanic had to spray it all the time so that it would turn. Runners were peeing on their hands to try and warm their fingers. The last ones up were riding in 20cm of snow.'

Jean-Claude Theillière, former champion of France, was there in 'that brutal, crazy thing. It is the worst memory of my life. Two hundred kilometres in rain and snow, and I only had a tracksuit jacket for protection. It was soaked through in 10 minutes. What was I supposed to do? I only weighed 57kg! The brakes stopped working. I fell two or three times in the descents. I know cycling's not for light-weights, but there were grown men crying.'

Marino Vigna was driving the Faema team car: 'The image which will stay with me is of Lake Misurina, the last false flat before you get to the real climb. The road was completely flooded. I could see Merckx in the middle of the road, riding through the water as if he were on a speedboat.

*1 June, 1968, Italy: Merckx braves the rain and snow after having
just won the 12th stage of the 51st Giro from Gorizia to Lavaredo*

Then, in the snowstorm, he caught the breakaway riders
one by one. His sister, by the side of the road, handed him a
bottle of hot tea, which he poured over his shoes to warm
his feet. The Arunzo refuge – a base camp for mountain-
eers – had been turned into a field hospital. People had
paralysed fingers, frozen toes, hypothermia. Gimondi was
in shock, he was crying. He knew his chance had just gone.
And that is the story of the first of Merckx's five Giros.'

But there is another side to every story. This one
was revealed in a book written by Beppe Conti, now a
journalist for RAI, in homage to Enrico Peracino, who
was doctor for first the Carpano team and then Faema.
Giacotto – the manager – and Dr Peracino went back
a long way as friends and accomplices. Out of simple

curiosity, and because his admiration for Merckx seemed to know no limits, Giacotto asked Peracino to undertake an electrocardiogram on him, to 'see how the heart of a phenomenon works.'

The 1968 Giro started in Campione, Como, and arrived in Alba on the third stage. As decided, Giacotto, Peracino and a cardiologist from their entourage, Professor Giancarlo Lavezzaro, offered Merckx a routine check-up. The result hit like a guillotine blade, and was, according to Lavezzaro, 'stupefying'. He said to the other two: 'This man could have a heart attack at any moment.' Panic stations. Not a word to Merckx. The three of them didn't rule out some kind of handling error so decided to perform another ECG the next day before the start of the stage. Just to be sure, Adorni took one too. The result was the same as the previous day. Neither Giacotto nor Peracino had the courage to inform Merckx, so he continued on the Giro.

In the meantime, Professor Lavezzaro went back to work at the Molinette hospital in Turin. A student of the renowned cardiologist Professor Bruscha, he showed him the ECG results, without revealing the patient's identity. Bruscha asked him, 'Whose heart attack is this?' Further examination revealed that Merckx had hypertrophic cardio-myopathy. It would not prevent him winning at Tre Cime di Lavaredo and from keeping the pink jersey until the end.

Gianni Motta's memory is also invaluable. In Cassano d'Adda in the greater metropolitan area of Milan – where he lives – Motta is more than just a name, and much more than just the winner of the 1966 Giro. The octogenarian is part of the landscape, and his words – his lively personality – add depth to even the smallest anecdotes. A sunny, charming character, he does not dodge any questions. With him, nostalgia brings a breath of fresh air to yesterday's world. He was also there at Lavaredo, 'a survivor. I can still see myself saying to Gimondi, who was lying on a bed, sobbing, "you aren't going to beat Merckx by crying like a child".'

Motta and the five-time winner of the Giro would challenge each other in races across all types of terrains for 10 years. With great self-assurance, he asserts: 'Eddy was more afraid of me than he was of Gimondi. He never knew when I was going to attack. Sometimes I didn't even know myself. I was always coming up with new things, like Leonardo da Vinci. Downhill, he was better than everyone else, but he never dropped me. On top of all his qualities, we must acknowledge one great merit: for our generation, he provided extraordinary motivation and was an example. How many times did I wake up in the morning and tell myself: if you want to win you have to beat the strongest. Merckx was the strongest, so to beat him I had to use cunning. But I often lacked a bit of luck or a bit of strength. The poet says it better than me: "sometimes the wine is lacking, sometimes the cup." I tried everything; I even tried to buy the race. In the Tre Valli Varesine in 1970 we were the leaders, and I said to him:

"Eddy, we're in my country, let me win."

"No."

"But you've already won 35 times and I'm just out of hospital. It would really help my morale. I'll give you 500,000 lire (£230)."

"No."

"One million, Eddy!"

"No."

"Two million!"

It went up to 3.5 million (£795) and he didn't even blink. So much the better for me as it turned out – I beat him in a fair sprint and saved my money. It was in his character; he was not for sale. I won't go so far as to call him incorruptible, because everyone knows he gave up a Coppa Agostoni to Gimondi, but the primary condition he set for himself was to serve no one.'

Motta's hands are gesticulating; it's as if he needs to speak. He laughs loudly and thinks for a few seconds before he gives his opinion on what separated him from Merckx: 'he was a man of character, I was a man of destiny. He was meticulous, an obsessive perfectionist. He was utterly rigorous. I, however, believed in my lucky star. Eddy entered the Giro with 11 bicycles, frames at different angles, long forks, short forks and about 10 pairs of shoes. I laughed a lot at Adorni's story from the 1968 Giro: Eddy arrived with three suitcases and Vittorio asked him, with just a touch of irony, "Where are you going on holiday?" It was an era of one-up-manship. Competition was ruthless between the brands, and in Italy large sums of money were handed out – under the table – to secure a victory. There were two big, well-known buyers: Colnago and Salvarani. The Statute of Limitations has passed, I think I can say it. Do you know what the four Salvarani brothers' team was known as? The suitcase team.'

One year later, in the 1969 Giro, the biggest scandal in the history of Italian cycling occurred: the Savona affair, which led to Eddy Merckx's expulsion from the race following the result of a positive doping control the day before. Coincidentally, he had, just two days earlier, refused a suitcase full of money to lose the Giro.

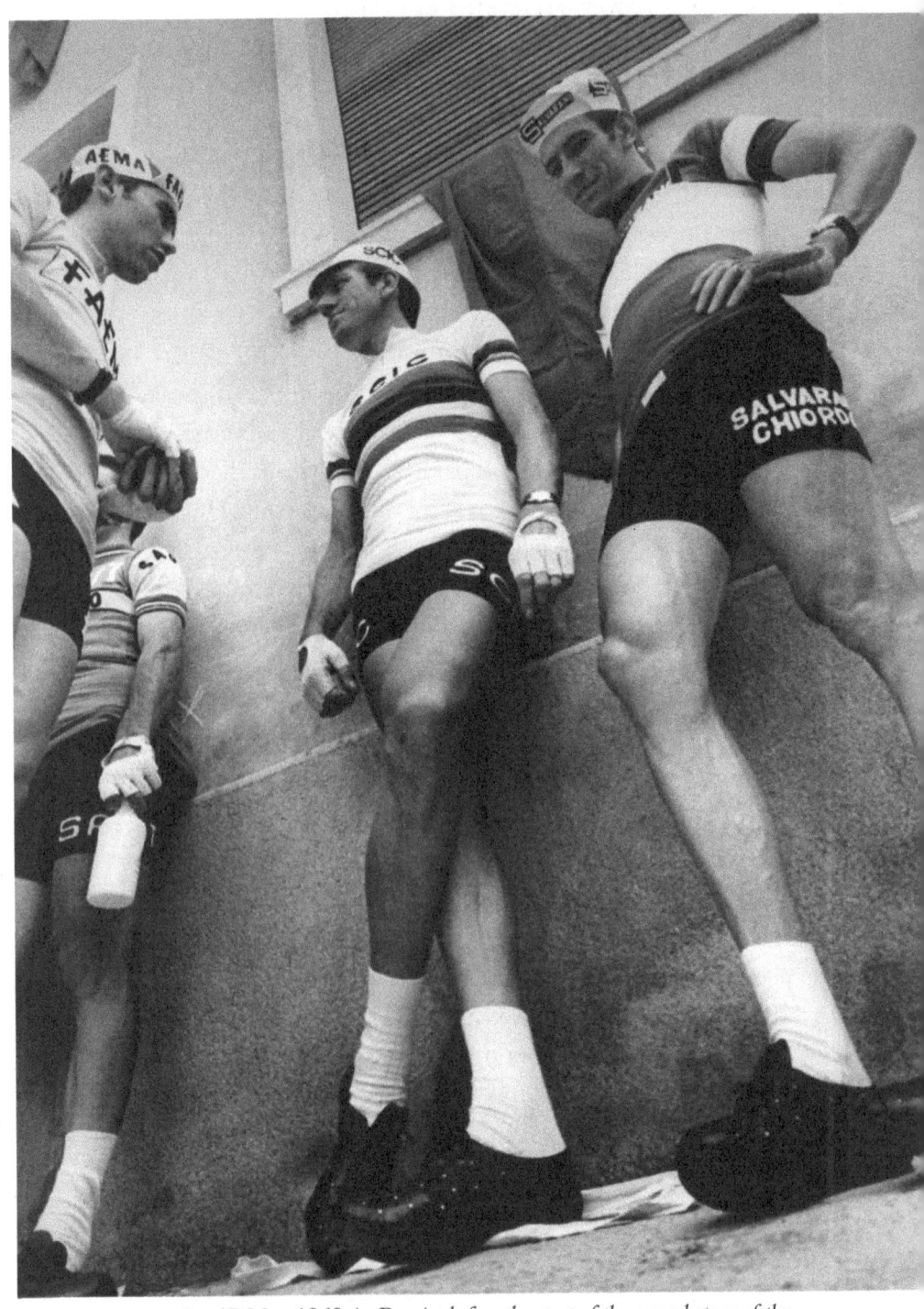

On 17 May 1969, in Brescia, before the start of the second stage of the Giro d'Italia, Eddy Merckx (L), Vittorio Adorni (C), and Felice Gimondi (R) are deep in conversation. The bombshell from Savona is still a long way off

SAVONA:
A MURKY AFFAIR

'In 2004, Ercole Baldini told me: "I've got all
the details about the Savona drug test. Who did
it. How much. If Eddy wants to know, have him
call me." I phoned Eddy and told him. At the
end of the line there was silence, then he said:
"I've already taken plenty of revenge. It's OK.'"

MARINO VIGNA, EDDY MERCKX'S

DIRECTEUR SPORTIF

Eddy Merckx tested positive three times in his career.
Twice in Italy. The first time was in 1969 during the Giro
d'Italia when Merckx tested positive for Fencamfamine, a
stimulant related to Reactivan. It was a murky affair that
beggars belief, blending lies and intrigue in true *combinazi-
one* fashion. Then again in 1973 at the Tour of Lombardy,
for Norephedrine, which had been mistakenly prescribed
by his doctor to treat the onset of bronchitis. The third
time came in Belgium at the 1977 Flèche Wallonne, where
he tested positive for Stimul, a popular amphetamine that
was widely used across the peloton at the time. Disqualified
from the Giro in Savona, he was later cleared due to the

benefit of the doubt, and the glaring procedural errors. His good faith was also acknowledged at the Tour of Lombardy, although he was stripped of his first-place finish in favour of Gimondi. However, his arguments were not accepted in the case of the Flèche Wallonne, and he was stripped of his third-place finish.

Of the three it is the Savona affair that continues – more than 50 years later – to fuel all sorts of speculation, some of it pretty ugly. So, what exactly did happen at the end of the 16th stage that departed Parma at 11 a.m. on that sunny day? It is hard to work out what really went on, because so many of those present at that Giro have disappeared. But it is definitely true that it is one of the most unlikely, most unbelievable and most staggering doping cases. It reads like something from a novel. Everything is shrouded in doubt. From the morning mass, which was celebrated at Parma Cathedral in honour of the Giro, where Merckx, wearing the pink jersey, rode with his teammates, right up to the doping control six hours later, which took place in a mobile caravan after the arrival in Savona.

Merckx had undergone eight tests since the start of the Giro in Brescia, either because of stage victories or because of the pink jersey. Montecatini (3rd stage), Terme (4th), Terracina (7th), Potenza (9th), Campitello Matese (10th), Scanno (11th) and San Marino (14th and 15th) – all negative. Why would he have made a massive error on the 16th day, on a flat stage that offered little difficulty and zero risk of him losing the pink jersey? In the Faema camp they were convinced, 'Merckx was set up.' *Directeur sportif* Marino Vigna is still convinced to this day. Questions abound. First up is the reliability of the portable caravan where the anti-doping control was carried out. According to Vincenzo Giacotto, the Faema team manager, security was 'rough and ready'. A crucial point of the regulations was not adhered to and he pointed it out straight away to Vincenzo Torriani, organiser of the Giro: 'A mobile lab has to be in place for a period of three months in the same location without moving before it gets approval. That was the first offence.'

Moreover, 'the bottles used to collect the urine were already open when the riders arrived, and they weren't sealed in the presence of the individual concerned' – another point that's absolutely contrary to correct procedure. And then there were all sorts of people simply hanging around who had nothing to do with the testing. But the first two weeks were uneventful. Giacotto finally said to himself that he might have been worried for no reason.

Savona, Sunday 1 June, 1969: no sooner had Roberto Ballini of team GBC won the sprint than right behind him, Eddy Merckx was already at the mobile lab, eager to get back to the hotel. Merckx was emphatic, the detail important: the doctor doing the control handed him 'a test tube that had already been unsealed, just like the other days.' Myself and Robert Janssens discussed it with his roommate Martin Van Den Bossche. 'Eddy had already won four stages and the atmosphere was pretty relaxed to be honest. The day before, his wife Claudine had been to visit. His morale was high. On the road to Milan he had a clear run – he was on course to win his second Giro. What's the worst that could happen, apart from a fall?' At the Albisola hotel, in the heart of the old town of Savona, there was nothing to report. The evening passed calmly and the next day they would be in Pavia after a flat stage. A day for winning. Milan had never seemed closer.

Savona, Monday morning, 2 June: the usual rituals, the usual habits before setting off on a stage. After breakfast, Merckx and Van Den Bossche went back to their room. Outside it was already hot. Stretched out on the bed in their cycling shorts, it was the last moment they had to relax. But Eddy was never caught off-guard, he was always alert. The only thing left to do was put on the pink jersey. Martin also remembers that 'we were disturbed twice. First there was a knock at the door and it was opened immediately. A woman wanted an autograph, then another one a second later. I told Eddy, "the next one gets my pillow in the face!" There was another knock, but this time it wasn't another admirer, it was Giacotto, so he got a pillow in the face. But nobody had time to laugh. He was talking to Eddy, and I can still hear him saying it: "You can't go. You tested positive." Total shock. The words nearly knocked Merckx over. He replied, "It's impossible, I haven't taken anything."'

A muffled cry of rage. Tears. In the corridor, journalists who had been tipped off were already after a comment. In tears, Merckx repeated, like a robot: 'It's sabotage. I haven't taken anything, I swear.' It was ten in the morning and the *bomba Savona* had its first victim. Merckx was positive for the amphetamine Fencamfamine. He was thrown out of the race; Felice Gimondi was the new pink jersey.

Torriani, the boss of the Giro, was told about it during the night. At four in the morning, he called the president of the *Commissari Tecnici* panel and demanded an immediate retest. It was categorically refused. In essence, the jury president's response was: 'If Merckx starts, the Giro's over.' There were whispers that in the night someone had already informed the Salvarani brothers. Giacotto had to wait until 9 a.m. on the Monday. 'There had to have been someone behind it,' sighed Marino Vigna. Speculation was mounting. A mishap during Sunday Mass in Parma? Could someone have swapped bottles on the bikes while they were outside? 'Impossible,' Vigna insists. 'I had taken it with me just in case.'

Troubling events from before the Parma–Savona stage were revealed. Marino Vigna, a friend of Merckx as well as the *directeur sportif* knew about a murky exchange, which only looked worse in light of recent events. Here is his version: 'Two days before Savona, a foreign rider from an Italian team came into Merckx's room and said to him, "If you let Gimondi win the Giro you'll be given a suitcase with a large amount of cash in it."'

At this point I interrupted Vigna: 'Who was the rider?'

'He is no longer with us.'

'Fifty years on, you can tell us who he was then?'

'It was Altig. Rudi was the Salvarani team road captain. That kind of thing happened all the time.'

'What did Merckx say?'

Vigna laughs. 'Something along the lines of, "I don't want to know how much is in the suitcase – that way, I won't be able to regret it. Just tell them we're going all in." Altig did not insist. The really weird thing is, it didn't make us suspicious.'

Years later, Merckx made another troubling statement to Joël Godaert, journalist at Belgian newspaper *La Dernière Heure*: 'If you only knew how much Gimondi offered me for the world champion jersey in Mendrisio in 1971...'

But back to Savona. A rolling bomb does gather moss, you might say. The Savona affair reached as far as Belgian political circles and higher still, as King Baudouin looked into the matter – discreetly. The Belgian Foreign Minister demanded 'clarification without delay' from his transalpine counterpart. The Flemish Minister of Culture blamed 'the Italian Mafia for setting a trap.' The Belgian government even made the threat to suspend diplomatic relations. In the meantime, Eddy Merckx was suspended for one month, from 1 June to 1 July. The calculation was done quickly: The Tour de France, which started on 28 June that year, would start without him.

A battle of experts and lawyers began. The Faema team insisted on the right to see the spectrogram of its rider's urine. The Italian and Belgian federations deferred; that would be up to the International Cycling Union (UCI) to decide. No one got to see the results, and the procedural errors stacked up: the second sample was not unsealed in the rider's presence. The two test tubes of urine were then emptied. Marino Vigna, who knows a great deal about the ins and outs of the case, continues, 'Before leaving the hotel, 20 hours after the official control test, Giacotto, our manager, summoned other riders, *soigneurs*, mechanics and *directeurs sportifs* to conduct an anti-doping control test under the authority of a bailiff and in the presence of Prisco, Inter Milan's lawyer. Three journalists were there: Gianpaolo Ormezzano from the Italian newspaper *Tutto Sport*, Michel Seassau of *L'Equipe* and René Jacobs from *Les Sports*. That evening the samples were handed over to the Forensic Institute in Milan. There was no trace of amphetamine, which should remain present in urine for

48 hours. Merckx could not be sanctioned and the president of the Italian Federation, Adriano Rodoni, eventually lifted the ban, 'for the benefit of doubt.'

This outlandish affair, worthy of a cold case, resurfaced in 2004 during the Giro with a stage in Bormio. Vigna again: 'I had a call from Ercole Baldini to tell me: "I've got all the details about the Savona drug test. Who did it. How much. If Eddy wants to know, have him call me." I phoned Eddy and told him. At the end of the line there was silence, then he said: "I've already taken revenge many times. It's OK."'

*Luis Ocaña, Eddy Merckx and Cyrille Guimard (L to R) shake hands
after the second stage of the Tour de France in La Baule in 1972*

ORDUÑA:
12 MAY, 1973

'When I was making love, I had to think about
Merckx to really get going.'

LUIS OCAÑA, WINNER OF THE 1973
TOUR DE FRANCE

The threats, the insults, the spitting finally got the better
of Merckx. Too much hate. His growing unpopularity in
France – after four consecutive victories in the Tour –
combined with the very decent prize (for the time) of a
million pesetas (£5278) on offer from the organiser of the
Vuelta were enough to encourage Merckx to shift the focus
of his season to Spain and Italy in 1973. But the organisers
of the Tour de France still had hope. Maybe he would try
for all three Grand Tours?

For the first time Merckx lined up at the start of the
Vuelta a España. Critics on all sides were denouncing it
as a *Vuelta afeitada* – a 'trimmed' version, as they say in
Spain, when they talk of rigged bullfights after the bulls
'visit the barber' to have their horns filed down before
entering the arena. Ocaña focused his disappointment on
the lack of mountain stages. The exception was the Col

d'Orduña in the Basque Country, which was reputed to be steep and rough, but when compared to stages in the Pyrenees, the Alps or the Dolomites, looked like very little. Conversely, bonus seconds were distributed by the handful at each stage finish and in many *metas volantes* (intermediate sprints). Luis Ocaña was indignant: 'This Vuelta's route is a scandal. There are no mountains but there are bonuses left, right and centre so Merckx can win at a canter.'

Two events occurred at the end of March. The one on the 30th was a historic date for the champion of Spain. For the first time in his career he beat Merckx in a time trial. It took place during Catalan Cycling Week, between Vallvidrera and Molins de Rei over 13km and where 28 seconds separated them at the finish. Ocaña proclaimed: 'This is just the start of what awaits Merckx on the Tour de France.' At the beginning of the season Luis was flying. Wherever he went he made a splash: Catalan Cycling Week, Tour of the Basque Country, the Dauphiné. No one could stop him. He was brimming with confidence. Because he knew that there would be cobblestones in the next Tour de France, he lined up for the Paris–Roubaix (another first), which was won by Merckx in the cold, rain and mud. Ocaña was half an hour behind, finishing in 29th position, but he was jubilant: 'I'm tougher than people think.' He was even more confident thinking of the July sun: 'And this time I'm going to get him, that Cannibal prick.'

Luis knew that people loved his verve, his fighting spirit, his way of making music of his words – images that only he could come up with. For example: 'When I made love, I forced myself to think of Merckx in order to really get going,' is a quote from *Perdants Magnifiques* (Magnificent

116

Losers), Xavier Garcia's brilliant book. We're heading into psychosexual-cycling-hangup territory, but no matter, what it boiled down to was that Merckx really drove Ocaña off the rails. But in Luis's words there was evidence of his need for revenge, his lust for life, his tendency to rebel. Ocaña almost made it a purely Spanish question, involving honour, jealousy, misery – or even the Civil War that his father (also Luis) fled.

Ocaña had just lost the Tour de France twice in a row. He crashed on the Col de Menté in 1971, where a memorial stands on a bend of the descent to mark that tragic Monday 12 July. Antoine Blondin immortalised that day in print: 'On this Tour, Ocaña may not have been the best, but he was certainly the star.' He suffered again in 1972, that time forced to abandon the race because of pneumonia. He swore there would not be a third time. He even vigorously challenged the arguments of his employer, Christian Darras (marketing director of Bic), who explained, 'That crash on the Col de Menté was the best thing that could have happened to our company from an advertising standpoint. After that, Luis was like some Greek tragic hero, admirable and admired by the general public, and light years from Merckx the ogre.' The Spanish journalist Carlos Arribas made reference to the fact that the *Hidalgo* is proud. In Spain it is well known that a tough man always gets back up, because '*los españoles, todo lo saben resolver por cojones, y tu eres uno, Luis.*'[19] Ocaña knew, however, that in spite of this popular, flowery and downright macho maxim, even if he gave it his all it would not be enough to solve his Merckx problem.

The second event occurred at the end of Catalan Cycling Week, where he again beat Merckx. That he won was not

---

[19] 'Spaniards are people who solve everything with their balls – and you are one of them, Luis.'

that extraordinary in itself, although it did come in a Classics campaign that "the ogre" was dominating: he'd won Liège–Bastogne–Liège (for the fourth time), Paris–Roubaix and Gent–Wevelgem (third time), Omloop Het Volk (second time) and the Amstel Gold Race for the first time. But the news that Merckx announced in Catalonia was a hammer blow that stunned Luis. His eternal rival, his sworn enemy – the one who would extend a hand years later to pull him out of trouble – had officially announced that due to the hostile atmosphere he would not be contesting the Tour de France that year. At first Ocaña thought it was a bluff, but pretty soon it became clear it wasn't. After the Vuelta and the Giro, which started just four days later, Merckx would not compete in a third Grand Tour in a row. He would use the July break to prepare for the end of the season. At the end of the Vuelta, as provocation, he even gave his podium prediction for the forthcoming Tour: Fuente first; Zoetemelk second; Poulidor third. Ocaña was furious.

In that Vuelta, from 26 April to 13 May, 1973, between Calpe and San Sebastián, with the absence of José Manuel Fuente – the defending champion who chose instead to challenge Merckx in the Dolomites – everything unfolded just as Merckx had anticipated. After just a week, solely through the time bonuses, he was already almost two minutes behind. 'It was simple: Merckx would sprint whenever he saw a billboard,' said the Basque rider Txomin Perurena, an all-rounder who would go on to be King of the Mountains in the 1974 Tour, ahead of his compatriot José Luis Abilleira. But 'Peru', as he was known (and is missed by many), knew how to time his rides and always kept the best for last: 'Heading towards Bilbao Merckx was chasing bonus seconds in the *metas volantes* – flying sprints – as he did every day. The peloton was rolling along calmly, and suddenly Merckx attacked, to general incomprehension. He gained a 20m lead and was first under a banner that was strung between two poles. It turned out that it wasn't a race marker at all, but a protest sign from the (then-clandestine) Communist Party, complaining about working conditions at a nearby factory.'

Ocaña scoured the Vuelta race book in every direction, hoping to find a window of opportunity. He found it in the 16th stage between Torrelavega and Miranda de Ebro, which was 203km long. It didn't really bother him that it came too late. Merckx was totally in control and could no longer be beaten. The next day was the final stop, in San Sebastián. On his road book, Luis had spotted the Orduña Pass: altitude 900m, 8km long, with an average gradient of 8 per cent, reaching up to 14 per cent at the top. It was there, on his own turf, that he would issue a man-to-man challenge to the leader of the Vuelta. It was a question of honour. He was ready to write his own legend: Hector-Ocaña versus Achilles-Merckx, unless you'd rather call it David-Ocaña versus Goliath-Merckx. Deep down, there remained a tiny spark to remind him of Orcières on the Tour de France in 1971. He knew that he could use that spark to set off a rocket, a full bonfire even. It was on the slopes of Orduña that he would make his final stand.

It seemed like the entire population of Vizcaya was gathered along the roadside to cheer for Ocaña. Through the hairpin bends of the pass, the energy of the Basque crowd was passionate. Under a winter sun that lit up the green slopes of the Sierra Salvada, Luis attacked. 'He wanted

Merckx to remember it,' is how it looked. At the top, the champion of Spain was all alone. Ahead of everyone. He got the better of 'the other one', as he sometimes referred to Merckx. What was there for Ocaña at the moment he crossed the pass to the other side, where Merckx – much better on the descent – would no doubt soon join him? 'Joy in my legs,' he said. And honour. The shadow of Don Quixote, looming large in the distance, was cast away.

In the Vuelta, Merckx nearly took it all: overall winner, six stage victories, points ranking and combination ranking. The only thing missing from his list of conquests was the mountains classification, snatched from him by José Luis Abilleira, a stubborn climber who trained all year in the passes of the Sierra de Guadarrama near Madrid. There are fond memories from the Castilian mountaineer: 'Merckx made it personal. Whenever there were points to be gained, he'd get his "motorbikes" going, he'd be on the wheel, and he would sprint up the climbs, hoping to leave me behind. He only shook my hand on the podium on the last day. That mountain jersey is the greatest honour of my career and my life. The following year during the Tour de France, he asked me if I wanted to join his team, but I had one year left with La Casera, and they didn't want to let me go.'

Luis Ocaña defied The Cannibal's prediction by crushing the 1973 Tour in the style of the man himself with six stage wins. The second-placed general classification rider, Bernard Thévenet, was 15 minutes and 51 seconds behind. But sometimes victory has a bitter aftertaste. Winning a yellow jersey without Merckx in the running just wasn't the same. It wasn't the one framed in his office, where he kept, like a relic, another yellow jersey - the real one, the one he really cherished. It was stained with blood and mud after his crash on the descent from Menté. Luis, who took his own life in 1994, never really came to terms with Eddy's absence that year. Over time, it turned into an obsession – a fixation, a missed chance to make history.

Merckx before the start of the third lap of
the Giro d'Italia at La Spezia in 1967

SAN REMO:
THE SEVEN-TIME WINNER

'Do you know many lotteries where the winning
number comes up seven times out of ten?'

EDDY MERCKX

The Cyclone that hit the Milan–San Remo between 1966
and 1976 should have been named Eddy. Eddy I, Eddy
II, Eddy III – all the way up to Eddy VII. Eddy Merckx
was 20 years old when he was crowned champion of *La
Primavera* – spring in Italian – for the first time, on Via
Roma in 1966. It was the first time he had taken part in an
international Classic, as well as the first time he had raced
further than 250km. He was wearing the white chequered
shirt of the Peugeot team and he was still just a young rider
who, with one bold leap, attained the seemingly unattain-
able. It was not some random roll of the dice. By the end
of that same season he had achieved two other prestigious
results: second place in the Tour of Lombardy – only a
manoeuvre by Vittorio Adorni kept him from victory – and
a win in the Trofeo Baracchi, where he was partnered with
Ferdinand Bracke. At the time of the winter break, Merckx
was the rider with the highest number of victories: 20 from

99 race days. Walter Godefroot, the champion of Belgium, had 16. Willy Planckaert, the Tour de France green jersey winner and Ward Sels, the Tour of Flanders winner, both had 13. Rik Van Looy, who was in decline, was on 12.

'Eddy II' repeated the feat in 1967, still in a Peugeot jersey. And although his rivals carefully scrutinised, watched and spied on his every move, he was in front at the top of Turchino, the first major climb that connects the Pô Valley to the descent towards the Gulf of Genoa. When Gianni Motta launched a sharp attack on the Capo Berta along the seafront, 50km from San Remo, Merckx was the first to chase him down. The peloton scattered. Motta was two years older and more experienced – more crafty, too. He had won the last Giro, and in this finale he was on his home training roads.

Sitting on his sofa 57 years later, between laughs and revelations Motta remembers the details of that particular moment: 'My instinct was warning me that there was someone behind, but there was no way I was turning around. I peeked under my elbow and I could see this white jersey about 300m behind me. I just knew it was Merckx. If he wanted to catch up with me he'd have to be strong, so I accelerated. The chase lasted 5km and we ended up side by side for the first – and certainly not the last – time. I knew nothing about him except that he had won the San Remo once. We were both confident and we immediately started working together without saying a word. It was a good understanding, right up to the foot of the Poggio. And there I saw just how strong he really was. At least 10 times he tried to drop me. Ten times I came back. And – as was common in those days – I negotiated. We were on the descent together and I don't even recall what we did to communicate. I told him "I want to win" and I'm sure he said "yes" back. I can't remember what I promised in exchange, but we seemed to be in tacit agreement. And suddenly, on Via Aurelia – probably alerted by the noise of the cars – we turned around and 50m behind us were Bitossi and Gimondi. At the fountain where the Via Roma begins there were four of us with just 300m to go. I launched a sprint on the right and Bitossi came across to squeeze me. A quick tap on the brakes. Just enough to make him lose a length – precisely the gap that separated me from Merckx on the line. We never talked about it again.'

Throughout this book, this question came up again and again: how could a rich, booming company the size of Peugeot in the 1970s let go of a rider of Eddy Merckx's quality? Why didn't they extend his contract, give him the Belgian crew he was asking for? I always got the same answer. Christian Raymond, author of the book *Cannibale*, explains with good humour, like something from a Michel Audiard[20] movie: 'Our *directeur sportif* Gaston [Plaud], had no separation between brain and stomach. He would rather be eating *foie gras gelée au porto* than discussing race tactics. At the wheel during a stage, he put on a show. But his job as *directeur sportif* came second to the evening's formalities. In addition to his Milan–San Remo victory in 1967, Merckx added the Gent–Wevelgem, the Flèche Wallonne and the rainbow jersey to his list of conquests. But it was

[20]Michel Audiard was a French director with an irreverent style akin to Quentin Tarantino

already too late, the split was final, and everyone knew Eddy was off to Italy.'

The first Classic of the season – first of the five Monuments on the calendar – is also the longest, at 300km. It was a distance that the seven-time winner quickly learned to master: 'I always arrived at the start of Milan–San Remo 100 per cent ready. The Giro di Sardegna (Tour of Sardinia), where I extended the stages, and Paris–Nice would not have been enough. I started my preparation in the winter with the Six Days. In 1966, I had competed in those in Gent and Brussels, and I added two Madisons – Rocourt and Roubaix. For trajectories, technique, reflexes – there's nothing better than the track,' he explained to journalist Robert Janssens. And he added: 'The 300km wall was key. If it was a 250km race there would be 20 more sprinters at the finish. But when it was 300, not many of us could cross that wall. In a sprint, with power, I had a good chance.'

No one else had that sixth sense like he did: to strike hard at just the right moment in just the right place. Most of the time this happened on the Poggio, where there was a balcony overlooking the sea at an altitude of 160m. The road climbs gently (3.7%) between the lemon groves, small workers' gardens, olive trees, abandoned greenhouses and Bussana church. Finally, there was the once-iconic TIM telephone booth. It had cult status but sadly fell victim to modernisation and was demolished under the orders of some pen-pusher in July 2023. As the final landmark before the descent, it had fuelled the dreams of many potential winners. While the climb, which is 3.7km long, has a bucolic feel, the opposite slope – with 23 hairpin bends – is wild and treacherous. Merckx made the difference on both sides of the slope, and he particularly excelled with his explosive style, just like Tomba *La Bomba*[21], in this unique 3km slalom.

In 1969, he left the RAI motorbike behind. 'I thought he was going to kill himself,' his manager, Giacotto, said after he finished. In 1972, Motta, who was really strong in the descent, was 12 seconds behind at the top, but never managed to bridge the gap. In 1976, a young newcomer, only 20 years old, caught up with him right at the telephone booth. Jean-Luc Vandenbroucke – a virtuoso in the pursuit – thought he had done the hard work only to find himself faced with a sudden, overwhelming challenge that tested him to the core. 'On the corners my pedals were scraping the tar and making sparks. I had never seen anything like it. But he didn't lose me.' He was happy to have made it that far, staying right on the wheel of Eddy VII. 'I didn't even dare contest the sprint. I sat up 200m from the finish – I wasn't even close.' Vandenbroucke would later learn he was disqualified after a positive doping test: 'They wanted to sabotage my career,' he said bitterly. 'The same thing happened to Eddy in Savona in the 1969 Giro. I swear on my children that I hadn't taken anything.'

The Belgian journalist Joël Godaert suggested to the seven-time winner that the race was a bit of a lottery, with no major difficulty. Eddy replied: 'Do you know many lotteries where the winning number comes up seven times out of ten?' While these successes brought joy, pride and happiness to the King of San Remo, the 1971 race was marked with tears, emotion and sadness. It involved the loss

---

[21] *La Bomba* was the nickname of Alberto Tomba, an Italian alpine ski champion famous for his explosive, aggressive style in slalom and giant slalom events.

of a friend. Merckx was in the process of winning Paris–Nice when news of Jean-Pierre Monseré's death reached him in his room in Saint-Rémy-de-Provence. Monseré had been struck by an oncoming car during a *kermesse* (festival) race in Retie on Monday 15 March. Four days later, Saint Joseph's Day – a Friday – Merckx was at the start of the Milan–San Remo. Monseré's funeral was set for the next day, in Roeselare. Eddy promised to attend and to place the winner's bouquet at the foot of the coffin. Race conditions were awful, cold and windy with icy rain. Roger and Erik De Vlaeminck, Monseré's teammates on the Flandria team, did not even make it to the halfway point. Merckx stuck with it and won. On Saturday morning he was in Roeselare with the bouquet from the Milan–San Remo. He paid his last respects to his friend, dead at 22 years old, at the peak of his powers.

A lot of water has flowed down the river Pô, times have changed and now the champions of the 21st century are measured in watts. But the Milan–San Remo continues to cast the same spell on the generations that come and go. At the beginning of the last century the Belgian Cyrille Van Hauwaert cycled from Moorslede, his home in West Flanders, to Italy. He said it was for training and he went on to win the 1908 race. Mathieu van der Poel, the 2023 winner, shared his 2021 Milan–San Remo data (he came fifth) on the mobile app Strava.

On the 3.7km climb up the Poggio, the Dutchman produced 497 watts over 5 minutes and 42 seconds. Tadej Pogačar and Wout van Aert also shared their statistics. According to Strava, they are the new co-holders of the climb record since 2023, achieving it in 5 minutes

36 seconds, at an average of 39km/h! The hill at Poggio, which first featured in the race's finale in 1960 as an unassuming mound, is, according to Alexandre Roos, a journalist at *L'Équipe* – 'a cemetery of dreams, where reality kicks in. Everyone knows every inch of it, and they all know where to attack: 1.5km from the summit after the slight flat at the sanctuary of Madonna della Guardia. That's where the Virgin Mary appeared to Giovanni Peri, a local peasant, in the 17th century. The Poggio does not always give in so easily.'[22]

Year after year, this gentle little monster is still captivating, and numerous documentaries have tried to unravel its mystery. The one made in 2019 by two cycling enthusiasts, Nicolas Loth and Laurent Galinon[23], brings a sense of tenderness and emotion to the magical little mountain. It has the power – in the space of five minutes – to catapult a rider to glory … or just ask them nicely to return the following year. Coincidence or not, in 2019 the winner was Julian Alaphilippe. Meanwhile, from his spot on the hill, Eddy Merckx, soaring like a Pegasus, was the undisputed master of the place, and would be for a long time still.

[22]*Les Monuments du Cyclisme* (The Monuments of Cycling), various, 2022
[23]Available at https://www.lequipe.fr/Velo-mag/Stories/Actualites/Poggio-la-colline-sacree/1236295

*Merckx was an expert in mechanics, insisting on measuring
the angles of inclination on his bicycle himself, calipers in hand*

MEERBEKE:
THE CLASSICS

'Merckx was sometimes so strong that we were
relieved to see him go.'

ANDRÉ DIERICKX, SECOND IN
THE 1972 TOUR OF FLANDERS

In the Classics – some of which are elevated to the rank
of Monuments – the peloton, just as the real world, is
governed by a Darwinian principle: fortune favours the
brave. In these one-day races, Eddy Merckx proved to be
the bravest more often than anyone else, consistently bold
and generous with his effort. He is still the one and only
rider with 19 Monument wins on his list of achievements.
He is what one might call a truly extraordinary champion,
and his name is forever associated with the history and
legend of Belgian cycling, just as the Béguinages[24] on the
UNESCO world heritage list are eternally linked with the
image of Flanders. None of the five Monuments escaped
him. His magnificent career features seven Milan–San
Remo wins, two Tours of Flanders, three Paris–Roubaix

[24]The Flemish béguinages are a series of 13 historical sites in the Flanders region of Belgium

victories, five Liège–Bastogne–Liège titles and two Tours of Lombardy.

But let's look at *De Ronde*, the Flemish name for the Tour of Flanders. A combination of hills and cobbled roads, many of which seem hidden under the cover of trees before they suddenly rear up under a cyclist's wheels, *De Ronde* is like something from a bygone era. Two natural elements give it the reputation it has: cobblestones and hills. First, the cobblestones. They are unforgiving and harsh, and so dreadful that one novelist described them as 'teeming with witches, flora and devil's sulphur.'[25] *L'Équipe* journalist Pierre Callewaert points out that the cobbles on *De Ronde* – known as *kasseien* or *kinderkoppen* in Flemish (literally 'children's heads') due to their size and resemblance to a youngster's skull – now have protected status. Cleaned up and reshaped if necessary, each one of these dreadful granite blocks tells a story of what Callewaert called the 'Madmen's Tour'. Second, the hills give *De Ronde* an extraordinary character. Their slopes are sometimes so steep that they are like walls, as in Geraardsbergen (Grammont), known to locals as 'the little town on the mountain'.

Frans Verbeeck, a tenacious, stubborn, relentless rider who finished second twice in Flanders, embodies the stereotype of the Belgian cyclist with a Flemish flavour. Never further down than ninth place in seven entries, his formula for riding the hills tells you a lot about the mentality of Flemish riders before the start: 'You have to attack, dig deep and want it more than anything else.' André Dierickx, another famous cobblestone specialist who finished second

[25]Joris-Karl Huysmans

in both *De Ronde* and Paris–Roubaix in 1972, was raised in the same tough school of cycling. He knew how to do everything on those roads, but his assessment had a fatalistic undertone: 'Merckx was sometimes so strong that we were relieved to see him go. He always used the biggest gears on the cobbles, 53 x 13, while we were going all out on 53 x 14 or 53 x 15.'

And there we are. Merckx won the Tour of Flanders twice (1969 and 1975) and finished four times in third place (1967, 1970, 1973 and 1974) in 12 entries. He was 23 years old when – on his very first attempt in 1969 – he steamrollered his opponents in the dreadful weather conditions. The north wind was freezing, it was raining heavily and the snow showers, which turned spectators into statues, made it feel like you were in something from a Georges Simenon novel. At the front, again accompanied by four Italians – Gimondi, Bitossi, Basso and Zilioli – Merckx took his turns without flinching. Then, on a gradual uphill more than 70km from the finish, he left the *squadra* behind. With the look of a hungry predator, facing a headwind and the driving rain, he charged forward. There was panic in the Faema car. Guillaume Driessens, *directeur sportif*: 'Are you crazy or what? Wait for the group.' Journalist Robert Janssens, who covered the race for the Flemish daily *Het Laatste Nieuws*, later had the privilege of knowing Merckx's response to Driessens. 'Bollocks!' The gap with his pursuers was widening. Gimondi, in second, was six minutes behind when he arrived in Meerbeke, Basso nearly eight. That feat of 'The Cannibal' remains one of the greatest ever in the history of *De Ronde*. A memory from Robert Janssens, regarding the mid-race controversy with Driessens, whom Merckx really didn't like much: 'At the time I said that even the local priest could have been their *directeur sportif.* A baker or a train driver could have replaced Driessens without any problem. Merckx didn't need anyone to tell him what the race tactics were. He did what he wanted, where he wanted, when he felt like it.'

The 1969 season was one of the best of his career (43 victories from 129 race days) and his campaign in the Classics, with the Milan–San Remo, the Tour of Flanders and Liège–Bastogne–Liège, was simply dazzling. A long period of dominance by Eric Leman (1970, 1972, 1973) would follow before Eddy Merckx repeated another incredibly successful performance in 1975. That day, after a breakaway of over 100km, he was accompanied by Frans Verbeeck, who had immense difficulty taking turns with him: 'When I went in front the pace dropped by 2 or 3km/h, but I was giving it my all. Merckx clearly saw that I wasn't pretending, and on the Bosberg he actually waited for me, which allowed me to secure second place. He was riding like a demon, and by the time we were going up Muur van Geraardsbergen, I had to shout at him to "ease up, I'm done!".'

'The Flying Milkman' – Verbeeck's nickname from his first profession – finished the race in agony, saying: 'I couldn't see 10m in front of me; my vision was blurred. To be safe, I didn't even drive home that evening.' In 1975, as in 1969, Merckx won those same three Monuments: Milan–San Remo, Flanders and Liège–Bastogne–Liège (the Amstel Gold Race was an extra in 1975). He had a total of 38 victories from 151 race days.

He would ride *De Ronde* two more times. In 1976 he got caught up in the main group and finished 17th. It was near the end of his career, although he didn't know it at the time. In 1977 he abandoned the race. Over the course of his 12 entries, 'the Great Merckx' only put his foot on the ground once on a climb. That was on the Koppenberg, the real terror of *De Ronde*. It is a medieval path once used only by carts, and features monstrous cobblestones and a gradient of 22 per cent in some sections. Walter Godefroot, the winner in 1968, came across it during a training ride in 1970. When he informed the race organisers of his discovery, he slyly made sure to add: 'I know a route that you'll like, but I will only tell you where it is after I retire. There's no way I'll race there.'[26] Delayed by a crash in the middle of the peloton in 1976, Merckx covered the rest of the Koppenberg's 682m on foot, bike in hand. The image went around the world. The Japanese daily *Mainichi Shimbun* published it one day with the caption: 'God descended among men.'

---

[26] *Bahamontes* magazine

12 April, 1970: Merckx crosses the finish line at
Paris–Roubaix, five minutes ahead of his nearest rival

ROUBAIX:
THE PERFECT WEDDING GIFT

'De Vlaeminck is on the ropes. Merckx is coming back. Merckx is stronger. Merckx is going to win... Merckx. Merckx. Merckx... Shit, it's the other guy.'

LUC VARENNE, ON THE MICROPHONE FOR RTB AT
THE FINISH LINE IN 1975

Paris–Roubaix is the epicentre of something within a season: a dream, a dread, a fantasy – a wedding present. When he married Claudine Acou on 5 December, 1967, Eddy Merckx, already world champion and winner of two Milan–San Remos, promised his new wife that he would gift her a win in the Paris–Roubaix. This cobbled Monument – certainly not paved with good intentions – is a feat of bravery: a long, chaotic journey that demands specific qualities, character and the ability to deal with the weather. Rain, mud, wind and dust all add to this springtime extravaganza, making the race even more beautiful. It is tailor-made for a Flemish rider, someone who thrives on those elements their entire life. And there are those prestigious names from the past – Lapize, Speicher, Leducq, Pélissier, Coppi, Bobet,

Forestier, Van Steenbergen, Cerami – who seem almost to float above Mons-en-Pévèle, Carrefour de l'Arbre, Tilloy-lez-Marchiennes and Camphin-en-Pévèle. Those are the five-star cobbled sections that can destroy a rider's will – and each one tells a story. These gladiators of the cobbles truly deserve a tribute. So, since 1996, in a style similar to the Hollywood Walk of Fame, brass plaques bearing the winner's name have been put up in the velodrome showers – the very place where riders come to wash away the traces of a battle that lasts more than six hours. Only once has the Paris–Roubaix deviated from the rule and immortalised two names – the first and the last in 1968: Eddy Merckx and Philippe Crépel from Lille.

On 7 April, 1968, four months after his wedding, The Cannibal gave his wife his first cobbled trophy as a wedding gift, thereby saving his Classics season. He went on to win two more, in 1970 and 1973, and in his 12 entries he always reached the finishing line at Roubaix. He has three victories, the same number as Rik Van Looy, but one less than Roger De Vlaeminck, his biggest enemy on the cobbles.

The 1968 race, windy and sunny, ventured for the first time on to a new cobbled section that had been unearthed by former world champion Jean Stablinski, a native of Valenciennes in France, on an abandoned mining site. La Drève des Boules d'Hérin (or Trouée d'Arenberg – Trench of Arenberg) didn't yet know that it was about to become the very epicentre of the Paris–Roubaix race, the legend of all legends. It's a *drève* (drive), a *trouée* (hole) or even a *tranchée* (trench). They're all striking names. It is 2400m of treacherous, mud-covered cobblestone, traversed since time immemorial: by the *Poilu*[27] in 1914, trudging behind a cannon pulled by an old *rocinante* (carthorse); by the black-faced miners who went to the bottom of the coal pits; by the peasants transporting cartloads of beetroot. Even by the young Stablinski, a former *galibot* (child miner) on his way back from the local dance on Sunday evening, his accordion on his back. But that was a thousand years ago.

For the riders, Paris–Roubaix and its cobbles are ragged territory. Both are wild, both can cause damage and both demand an unthinking, all-out effort. Merckx was up to the task, whatever the weather. In 1968 only Van Springel held him all the way to the velodrome and the sprint was a formality. Weakened by a sore throat the following year he finished second, losing out to the Flandria team's four-man block: Godefroot (the winner), the De Vlaeminck brothers and Leman. It was a similar scenario again in 1970: Merckx was up against four Flandria riders: the two De Vlaemincks, Leman and Dierickx. But this time in the rain, wind and mud he overcame the competition. 'The Gypsy', in second place, arrived in Roubaix more than five minutes behind. In France the first signs of annoyance surfaced. Jean Leulliot, the organiser of Paris–Nice and a columnist for *L'Aurore*, wrote: 'At this rate Eddy Merckx could well kill the sport of cycling.'

In 1971, Roger Rosiers, riding for the Bic team, won solo despite a crash and three punctures. Like a hussar on the cobblestones, and knowing full well he had to fend for himself, he explains: 'At the first feed zone, I had no teammates left to hand me a wheel if I got a puncture.

[27]French World War I soldiers

For a Frenchman, coming to race in Belgium or riding in the Paris–Roubaix with the crosswinds, jostling and bad weather, it was like punishment. But when I attacked at the end, not Merckx nor anyone else could follow me.' In 1973 the great Merckx was back. Rosiers says in admiration: 'It rained right from the start. Awful weather. About halfway I was part of a strong group: De Vlaeminck, Godefroot, Maertens, Verbeeck, Walter Planckaert and Van Springel – Merckx wasn't there. We came out of a cobbled section and on the tarmac the pace picked up to 60km/h, we had our heads down on the handlebars. We were pushing even harder to widen the gap. And just when we thought that was that, all of a sudden Merckx came up, eating a pancake. He had a smile on his face as if to say, "Did you forget about me?" We attacked one after the other to make him crack, but it was us who broke. He just went on as far as he wanted to. In the big moments, no one could rival him. He was simply too strong.'

No one, apart from one: Roger De Vlaeminck. In 1974 'The Gypsy' had got the better of Moser. Out of provocation, and because he didn't much care for the Italian, he replied to a journalist: 'The only thing that hurt were the blisters on my hands.' In the next race he had come to challenge Merckx, who had enjoyed a stunning spring of Classics: Milan–San Remo, Tour of Flanders, the Amstel Gold Race and soon Liège–Bastogne–Liège. The future five-time Tour winner ended up in a small lead group in the finale, alongside Dierickx, Demeyer and De Vlaeminck. As they came into view of the first houses in Roubaix, Merckx got a puncture. But he re-joined the group almost immediately, and it was the four of them that entered the velodrome. In the press box Luc Varenne, the famous radio reporter for RTB (Radio-Télévision Belge), was hyping it up. A former member of the French Foreign Legion who was passionate and loquacious, he was also an actor and worked on *Tintin* magazine. He was one of Eddy Merckx's greatest supporters. He was enthusiastic, sure that Eddy was about to win his fourth Paris–Roubaix. As the riders approached the finish line on the final sprint, he was commentating: 'De Vlaeminck is on the ropes. Merckx is coming back. Merckx is stronger. Merckx is going to win... Merckx. Merckx. Merckx... Shit, it's the other guy.'

The winner would hold it against him for a long time, but that's not what really mattered. The important thing was that these two 'monsters' were now tied at three wins each: 1968, 1970 and 1973 for Eddy; 1972, 1974 and 1975 for Roger. Their destinies intertwined. There was a touch of ego – only to be expected – but there was no jealousy between them. The two best Classics riders appreciated and respected each other. The dream of a fourth cobbled trophy took shape. In 1977, it was match point, and the sublime took over. Like an angel in black, De Vlaeminck skimmed across the stones, a 55km feast of cobblestones his favourite earthly fare. He weaved his way above the legend. He became the first rider ever to win the race four times.

In Kaprijke, at home in his living room, he lifts something up and taps it to his head. How beautiful a cobblestone can be! In his hands it looks like a sceptre, a jewel – a work of art.

Merckx (L) and Louis Pfenninger (R) at the head of the peloton

LIÈGE:
LA DOYENNE

'I was whistled at, insulted and threatened by 19,998 people; the only two who were on my side were my father and mother who had come with me by car.'

ROGER DE VLAEMINCK

Sitting on a black sofa, Eddy Merckx talks to Belgian journalist David Lehaire. With a rugged face, a forehead furrowed by the passing of the years and two deep lines running from nose to mouth, he radiates a quiet sense of calm – the kind earned over countless kilometres in the saddle. Conversation is fluid and sweeps across current events. Conducted in April 2024, the interview is on the DH Les Sports+ website. When it comes to his preference, for example, between the Tour of Flanders and Liège–Bastogne–Liège, Merckx doesn't pause for a second: 'Liège, because it was the hardest. The most consistent.' And he confirms: 'It was my kind of terrain. Plenty of hills and bad weather.' Five victories, one second place and one third out of 10 entries – no one has done better.

Some years, the Ardennes Classic – also known as *La Doyenne* – is still in the midst of winter when its time comes around on the calendar. On the way to Bastogne, where the temperature is a few degrees lower, the peloton is plunged deep into the Ardennes with its thick forest of fir, oak and birch trees. It is the country of coal and loggers. Of deer. *La Doyenne* is the soul of Walloon cycling. Sometimes snow leaves traces that never fade completely. In 1980 they renamed it 'Neige–Bastogne–Neige'[28] because of that year's particularly harsh weather, when the peloton faced near-freezing temperatures and a terrible snowstorm. That year's winner, Bernard Hinault, had his fingers frozen and still bears the scars.

These roads and landscapes bore the weight of the Great War and are classified among the natural wonders of the Ardennes. It was through here in 1914 that the German army advanced, led by Von Bülow, Moltke and Schlieffen. Twenty-five years later they came again in tanks. Every year, hundreds of cycle tourists set out to conquer these savagely beautiful hills: the Mur de Stockeu, where a monument to Eddy Merckx stands; the Côte de Wanne, from where The Cannibal launched a fantastic exploit in 1969; and the Haute Levée. As they approach Liège, the challenges unfold one after another like beads on a rosary: La Redoute, Les Forges (a tribute to Stan Ockers who won in 1955), La Roche-aux-Faucons and the final limestone climb up to Liège itself. The history of *La Doyenne* is inspiring, captivating and fascinating. A journalist, whose name I was unable to unearth, claimed that this 'Classic brings beauty to what

---

[28] *Neige* means snow in French

is otherwise just nature.' Its enduring popularity can be measured in three ways: by the list of prestigious names that grace its roll of honour; the endless lines of amateur cyclists that appear as soon as the weather is good; and by the number of pubs. The latter is an unconventional unit of measure, perhaps, but one that gave Jean-Baptiste Baronian, author of the *Dictionnaire Amoureux de la Belgique*, the brilliant idea of a 'Beer Route', in the way Wine Routes exist in France. At the refreshment stop, cyclists find comfort in the local brews, which carry picturesque, almost enchanting names: Vapeur en folie (crazy steam), Satan Red, Queue de charrue blonde (blond plough-tail), Marquise foncée (dark marquess), Hercule à vapeur (Hercules on steam), Poiluchette blanche de Thy (hairy wheat beer from Thy), Écume des jours (Froth of the days) and so on.

The first of Eddy Merckx's five victories came in 1969. His creative boldness and ambition had already made a mark: at Milan–San Remo three times, on the Tour of Flanders, at Roubaix. 'The Ogre' (his second nickname) loved to win more than anything else, but he didn't want ordinary victories. It was suggested that, like Julius Caesar, he would rather lose in style than win a cheap, mediocre or insignificant victory. What Merckx truly favoured were great, stylish attacks, full of panache and that swept all before them. When he launched his decisive attack on the Côte de Wanne there was still more than 100km of the race to go. Only his teammate Victor Van Schil could keep up with him – and even he found the finale too much. Merckx encouraged him, 'Hang on, Vic! Eat a little.' He even went so far as to wait for him. The two Faema teammates reached the Rocourt velodrome with a comfortable lead of eight minutes. Merckx even had time to provide commentary on the sprint for third place (Barry Hoban) into the BRT microphone. Another version, recorded in *Bahamontes* magazine, tells the epic story of Merckx and Van Schil (now deceased) differently. Rik Van Puymbroeck, a journalist, sourced some credible testimonies and claimed that before entering the cinder track Merckx reportedly asked his teammate, 'Vic, do you want to win?' To which Van Schil, ever the loyal companion, reportedly replied, 'What? No way! Even if you take a tumble I'll carry you myself so that you cross the line first.' Fact or fiction, who can really say?

On 17 April, 1970 at the start in Place Saint-Lambert in Liège, Merckx was once again the overwhelming favourite. On the cobblestones of the Paris–Roubaix he put on a masterful display, pushing his great rival Roger De Vlaeminck back by more than five minutes. He would also be the strongest in Gent–Wevelgem and the Flèche Wallonne, both contested after *La Doyenne* in 1970. There were six contenders for the win in the narrow corridor leading to the velodrome. Merckx, watchful and confident, had the cheese in his beak like the crow in the fable. In that story, there was only one fox, but here there were two De Vlaemincks. The other three in the breakaway, Verbeeck, Van Springel and Pintens, no longer had the big prize in their sights. On the final turn before entering the track, everyone was expecting a sprint, when all of a sudden only Roger De Vlaeminck appeared wearing the Belgian champion's jersey. He was a good few seconds ahead of the others. A lap and a half of the track further on and he had taken first place. What happened? Merckx accuses the brothers of tricking him. 'Erik, who was leading, pushed me to the left, almost into the ditch, and Roger shot off.'

During my meeting with 'The Gypsy' at his home in Kaprijke, the accused was happy to give his version of events. On an A4 sheet of paper, with careful precision, he drew the final bends of the tunnel, showing three nearly touching circles: 'The road wasn't wide. Just a little bigger than this table, maybe 3m. Erik was in front, on the left side, Merckx on his wheel. I was on the right. It all happened in a flash. I made a sign to my brother, he closed the door on Merckx and I made my move.' We can't review the footage as there was no camera at that spot, but what Merckx accused them of is part and parcel in a race, not an infraction. 'If he'd been more attentive, he'd have been riding in the middle not on the left. It was so narrow that the slightest mistake would make you kiss your chance goodbye. I think he was more annoyed than disappointed. But at that time we were truly at war with each other. At a criterion in Denderleeuw there were 20,000 spectators. I was whistled at, insulted and threatened by 19,998 people; the only two who were on my side were my father and mother who had come with me by car. I am not afraid of much, but all that hatred at the age of 20 … yes, I found it disturbing.'

The Cannibal made up for it in 1971 – 'Merckx' style. Ninety kilometres of freezing cold breakaway in the snow. He paid it no heed. He advanced fearlessly like Jupiter, because he knew he was the master of all storms. He brought his fellow countryman Pintens, who was with him in the finale, to the second step of the podium. In 1972, wearing the rainbow jersey, he started at Stockeu and rode solo to Verviers, where the finish line was. He added a fourth star to his 1973 list of honours, where, back in the velodrome again, he edged out the indefatigable Frans Verbeeck by just... 3cm. Finally, in 1975, after his victories in the Milan–San Remo, the Tour of Flanders, the Amstel Gold Race and a second-place finish in the Paris–Roubaix, he capped his Classics season with a final success in Liège, where Bernard Thévenet played it smart in the final. The Frenchman explains: 'I was well-placed in a group, with lads who were all faster than me. Merckx, Godefroot, De Vlaeminck, Dierickx, Verbeeck. Us French riders – Danguillaume, Delisle, Seznec and I – didn't count for much. But after six and a half hours of riding with all those sprinters watching each other, I said to myself: "If I launch a strong attack at the 1km mark, who's going to follow?" Because whoever chases me knows they've lost. On the Boulevard de la Sauvenière, I attacked as planned, but who caught up with me with 300m to go? Merckx, of course. And in the sprint I finished second.'

It was the 18th and penultimate Monument of his career. The last one was in 1976, in San Remo.

It's not enough to refer to him merely as some kind of sacred monster, a shining light or a symbol of the 1970s. How to put it? He could be Hemingway's hero, who 'In his great moments, hit the moon with his forehead.'

*In the finale of the Belgian Classic in Gand–Wevelgem on
1 April 1970, Merckx launched a decisive attack and won solo*

Gimondi, Merckx and Adorni (L to R)
on the podium after the 1968 Giro d'Italia

LOMBARDY: 1971–1973: GIMONDI, MAERTENS AND THE *BOMBA DI COMO*

'It's hard to face an opponent you know is better than you, but I don't believe there was any greater motivation than racing against Merckx.'

FELICE GIMONDI, WINNER OF THE
TOUR DE FRANCE, THE GIRO D'ITALIA
AND THE VUELTA A ESPAÑA

Twice, in both 1971 and 1972, Eddy Merckx bookended the season in his quest for the Monuments: Milan–San Remo and the Tour of Lombardy. In both cases he completed the picture with a victory in Liège–Bastogne–Liège. When he set foot in Lombardy in early October 1971, the man from Brussels had already earned 54 victories in 120 race days, and, in 1972, 50 victories in 127 competition days. The fatigue from a season that sometimes neared 200 days of racing was the first obstacle he had to overcome. But that was not a problem for him. The rain, fog, autumn cold and the unforgiving terrain of Schignano, the Passo d'Intelvi (a real 16km-long mountain pass), the Ghisallo or the Sormano Wall presented a much more formidable barrier.

Generally, on the first pass through Como – with still over an hour of the race to go – about 100 riders would turn off towards their hotels and shower. Merckx was never even tempted. 'He rode as if he had armour on; nothing could touch him,' said journalist Willem Van Wijnendaele. In 1979, Bernard Hinault drew inspiration from Eddy's method to triumph following a breakaway launched some 150km from the finish, alongside his teammate Bernard Becaas. They didn't even bother with the Italian Silvano Contini, who was unable to take a turn at the front. Almost at his peak in 1974, Bernard Thévenet, who finished sixth at 1 minute 24 seconds behind winner Roger De Vlaeminck, succinctly summarised the 4500m of elevation gained between Bergamo and Como with this concise phrase: 'Lombardy is mountains, courage and mental strength.'

In his tireless pursuit of victories, Merckx could have doubled his tally in *Classica delle foglie morte* ('race of the falling leaves'), bringing it to four wins. The first time he entered, in 1966, he was the fastest of the six survivors who rode into the Sinigaglia velodrome. Between Poulidor, Anquetil, Dancelli, Adorni, Gimondi and him, the sprint was surely a formality. But on the concrete track he made the rookie error of hugging the inside line. That wily old fox Adorni – Gimondi's teammate – didn't need to be asked twice. Half a lap from the finish, riding side by side with Merckx, he spread his elbows and then, shoulder against shoulder, unscrupulously shoved him, nearly sending the Belgian sprawling on to the grass of the football pitch. When Merckx did manage to get past Adorni on his right and launch his sprint, Gimondi was 15m ahead. On the line, Merckx missed out by half a length. No objection was raised: 'It's my fault – I did it to myself,' Merckx acknowledged. Black-and-white images in the INA[29] confirm Adorni's manoeuvre was more than dubious; he clearly obstructed his opponent and did not keep his line – a foul according to the rules.

That was Eddy's first confrontation with Felice Gimondi. The two men would meet seven times on the steep slopes of Lombardia. A race within a race. The man from Bergamo won in 1966 and 1973, the man from Brussels in 1971 and 1972. And in their back and forth, Merckx and Gimondi made it on to the podium three more times each: second in 1966 and 1974 then third in 1968 for Eddy; Felice was second in 1967 and third in 1970 and 1972.

The 1971 season was a good one for The Cannibal: he won the Milan–San Remo, Liège–Bastogne–Liège and the World Championship in Mendrisio – where he beat Gimondi. The two opponents met a week later in Lombardy for a rematch. Merckx was motivated. The doubts surrounding his victory in the 1971 Tour, which arose after Ocaña crashed in the Col de Menté, were not entirely dispelled. In winter conditions he left his nearest pursuers more than three minutes behind. Gimondi could only manage ninth place. The 1972 season was a carbon copy of the previous one. Merckx started with a fifth success in *La Primavera* and ended with the *Classica delle foglie morte*. In between the two, he managed another Liège–Bastogne–Liège. For the second time he won a Giro d'Italia–Tour de France double, which he would bring up to three in 1974. In Como he crossed the finish line 1 minute and 24 seconds ahead of Guimard and Gimondi. Only 17 riders were classified. The man was simply gargantuan. In two weeks' time he would fly to Mexico and attack the hour record, breaking it and setting the new mark at 49.431km/h.

[29]Institut Nationale de l'Audiovisuel (France's National Audiovisual Institute)

At the 1973 Tour of Lombardy, one week after the Montjuïc UCI Road World Championships – won by Gimondi – there were still scores to settle. Merckx and Maertens each accused the other of causing them to lose. They didn't talk for 30 years. Merckx was angry about everything the press reported. They questioned his integrity and insinuated that the battle between accessory suppliers Campagnolo (his and Gimondi's sponsor) and Shimano (Maertens's sponsor) influenced the finish. He swore that they got it all wrong, but the damage was done. And when Merckx gets angry, things really get shaken up. The race – rampage, more like – was a bloodbath. The opposition was ripped to pieces. He crossed the line more than four minutes ahead of a small peloton of 22 riders, led in the sprint by Gimondi. The podium was majestic: Merckx, Gimondi, De Vlaeminck!

A month later, while Merckx (without taking a break) had begun his track season with the Dortmund Six-Day race, the *bomba di Como* went off. Traces of the banned substance Norephedrine were detected in his urine, confirmed by a second sample. A week earlier, after winning À travers Lausanne, Merckx's doctor, Angelo Cavalli, gave him Mucantil – a syrup usually prescribed to newborns – to stop the onset of a cold. No one doubted that it was done in good faith, especially since Norephedrine has no real stimulant or performance-enhancing properties. But the damage was done. Even though his doctor admitted full responsibility – 'it's my fault, all my own fault, I'm the only one to blame' – the UCI's technical commission still stripped Merckx of his victory in the Tour of Lombardy. To this day, Merckx still insists it remains 'one of the most beautiful' wins of his career.

It may just be pure coincidence, but his disqualification again benefited Gimondi – just as in the 1969 Giro and his positive test in Savona. We found some evidence regarding the elegant rider from Bergamo who passed away in 2019. In *La Gazzetta dello Sport*, the three-time winner of the Giro, the Tour de France, the Vuelta a España, Paris–Roubaix, Milan–San Remo and the controversial Montjuïc Road World Championships admitted that 'facing Merckx was setting out to conquer the impossible. He is, without question, the greatest of all time in our sport and thanks to him, I improved on every terrain. I will always remember that mythical stage of the Tre Cime di Lavaredo in the 1968 Giro. That day, I cried like a *bambino*, feeling so useless, overwhelmed and ashamed for my *tifosi*.' When questioned about the Savona affair, Gimondi maintained that in that Giro, 'Merckx had the race won. No one could have beaten him. I know everything that was said about me, about the team, but I was not responsible for any of it.' And furthermore: 'Of all his victories it was in the 1969 Tour de France that he impressed me the most. A display of strength and intelligence. Like he was in a class of his own. And when the two of us were in a breakaway together, like at the World Championships in Mendrisio, I already knew how it would end. In a head-to-head sprint, I didn't even have a ghost of a chance.' After his title in Mendrisio, the *Corriere Della Sera* ran the headline: 'Merckx World Champion. Gimondi beats the others.' 'It's hard to face an opponent you know is better than you, but I don't believe there was any greater motivation than racing against Merckx.'

*On 4 September 1971, Merckx beats Felice Gimondi
in the sprint and wins his second World Championship*

HEERLEN, MENDRISIO, MONTREAL: THE WORLD CHAMPIONSHIPS

'Gimondi offered me nine million francs if I let him win. He could have offered me double or triple – my answer would never have changed. It was no.'

EDDY MERCKX, ON HIS 1971
WORLD CHAMPIONSHIP WIN

Over 13 years, from 1965 to 1977, regardless of the scale and fullness of his seasons, Eddy Merckx did not miss a single World Championship. Out of 13 entries he won three rainbow jerseys: Heerlen (1967), Mendrisio (1971) and Montreal (1974). He abandoned only once, in Zolder (1969). Only five riders throughout history have won three world titles: Alfredo Binda, Rik Van Steenbergen, Óscar Freire, Peter Sagan and him. In fact, Merckx wore four rainbow jerseys if you include the one from Sallanches (1964) as an amateur, although he had nearly missed out on selection due to a scheme by the doctor of the Royal Belgian Cycling League for a so-called heart weakness. It would take an independent medical evaluation from Gent University Hospital to prove his fitness. A good omen or just simple coincidence, his first title was won under the watchful eye of Jan Janssen, who was crowned professional world champion the following day. Both were unaware that they would soon become major players in the 1967 World Championships.

Heerlen, 3 September, 1967: Eddy Merckx started his second and final season in Peugeot colours. He did not arrive at the start in the best condition. He was the victim of a fall at the Belgian Championship in Mettet, suffering a concussion that forced him to cut short his preparation. There were three main contenders that day. First, Gianni Motta, winner of the Tour de Suisse, who'd come sixth in the Giro. Italian newspapers reported that his preparation was based on that of astronauts before they go into space. Second, Jan Janssen, winner of the Paris–Roubaix, the Vuelta a España and the Green Jersey from the 1967 Tour de France. In Limburg he was on home turf. Third, Eddy Merckx, winner of the Milan–San Remo, Gent–Wevelgem (ahead of Janssen) and the Flèche Wallonne. Was he sufficiently recovered from his fall?

During our meeting with Motta in Cassano d'Adda, Lombardy, we obviously talked of the famous, if controversial, 'lunar' preparation, taken under the authority of Doctor De Donato, which was mocked and criticised: 'There was much false reporting about me and the credibility of the doctor, saying he used a non-pressurised flight simulator to force my body to absorb more oxygen, or that he used a centrifuge to get me used to rapid acceleration. All De Donato did was revolutionise my diet. For weeks, I only consumed liquids based on pre-digested substances:

fish, meat and plant matter. True, it did smell a bit strong when I opened a bottle during training, but I got used to it. A few years later in the Tre Valli Varesine, Eddy and I were both in the breakaway. We were talking side by side. He opened his bottle, took a swig and I recognised the smell of the food prepared by De Donato. I was pleased to see people were copying us. The last week before Heerlen, on Monday, Wednesday and Friday, I did 300km each day. I had three teammates along to help me. Each one would ride for 100km before easing up and the next would take over. In Heerlen, De Donato was still part of the team. My last test results were excellent and at the meeting the day before the race I told the others, "I'm going for it straight away. I'm not waiting for anyone." They thought I was crazy. There was 256km to ride! Five hundred metres after the start I was already in the lead.'

It didn't take Merckx long to catch up, and on the climb up to Ubachsberg the Dutchman Van der Vleuten, the Spaniard Saez, and the Briton Addy joined them. 'At the top of the climb I turned to Merckx and said, "How far ahead do you reckon we are?" "About 10 seconds," he replied. I said, "It's over. They won't catch up."'

The second protagonist was Jan Janssen. Trapped from the start, the Dutchman caught up with the breakaway after a 50km chase. Here is his version of events: 'In the finale our *directeur sportif* Maurice De Muer was at the side of the road. In the penultimate lap he gave me a small piece of paper on which he had written, "Change bikes. Need 13 teeth." I hesitated. I had just used up a lot of energy in the chase, and I did the sprint with a 14-tooth cog. With 200m to go I was on the right, on Merckx's wheel. I fell back so I wouldn't get boxed in, touched his rear wheel and lost a metre and a half. I made my way back, but I missed out by 30cm. It is one of the biggest disappointments of my career.' The conclusion of the winner, Eddy Merckx: 'I don't think Janssen's move is what caused him to lose. If you look at the images, there's nothing out of the ordinary. That's just an excuse.'

Mendrisio, 4 September, 1971: this title race must be placed in the context of the Tour de France, which was still fresh in everyone's minds. Would Merckx still have won if Luis Ocaña, in the yellow jersey, had not taken a tumble on the descent of the Col de Menté? Many people think not. Revenge was served in Switzerland. Merckx prepared with extra care. An altitude training camp in Abetone (1400m), Tuscany. Four days before the race, he did a 300km training ride – by himself. The next day he left Abetone and cycled to Monza, a distance of 200km. On Friday, he did another 150km loop on the Tour of Lombardy route, passing through Ghisallo. On Sunday, the race unfolded clearly. He went clear halfway through the race, keeping Gimondi, Polidori, Pintens, Mortensen and Guimard by his side – wary of the latter's sprinting ability. Merckx attacked again and found himself head-to-head with Gimondi. The Italian then allegedly offered him a very large sum of money to take second place. Was that true or just rumour? 'True' insisted Merckx in his biography. 'Gimondi offered me nine million francs (£1,202,349) to let him win. He could have offered me double or triple – my answer would never have changed. It was no.' What about Ocaña? He was never in the race. In the mind of The Cannibal, the score from the 1971 Tour had been settled.

But there aren't only good memories among his various World Championships. In fact, Montjuïc 1973 – where Gimondi won ahead of Maertens – is a very bad one. It would be 30 years before Merckx and Maertens reconciled during a reunion of former riders in Beaujolais. Merckx, in a breakaway, didn't understand why his compatriot attacked to join him but then refused to work with him. This allowed Gimondi and Ocaña to catch up. Maertens, suffering from cramps, still agreed to lead the sprint for Merckx, but nothing went as planned and Gimondi took the win. Harsh words were exchanged. 'Coward.' 'Sell-out.' Thirty years! Beaujolais has these virtues...

Among the disappointments, Yvoir 1975, on Merckx's and De Vlaeminck's home ground, also left a bitter taste. This account from Jean-Pierre Danguillaume, who won the bronze medal, provides a first glimpse into the Belgian fiasco. 'I attacked in the penultimate round and immediately had Vlaeminck on my wheel. He wouldn't pull a single metre. I eased up and who did I see riding off? Kuiper. De Vlaeminck didn't react, and the other rider just kept going, calmly extending his lead. It wasn't my job to do the work, it was up to the Belgians.' Danguillaume admits he didn't know that Merckx had fallen after an hour of the race and, weakened, had put himself to work for De Vlaeminck as best he could. Perhaps the latter lacked the reinforcements to lead the pursuit for Kuiper? That much was obvious, but whose fault was it? The day before, De Vlaeminck had corrected a Belgian journalist who brought up the argument that 'having 11 riders is still a significant additional advantage.' (As the reigning champion, Merckx gave the Belgian team the right to race with one extra rider.)

'Eleven? No,' said The Gypsy. 'Ten and a half if you're including Van Impe.' The next day, that wisecrack – widely reported in the press – came back to bite him in the finale. When he signalled to *Petit-Lucien*, usually a delightful character, and asked him to take a turn, Van Impe, annoyed, softly replied that he was going flat out. 'In the last lap I launched another big attack,' Danguillaume continues. 'I got to within 100m of Kuiper, but I had Zoetemelk, his teammate, on my wheel. As Thévenet was also in the mix, I thought he was going to attack. The finish was perfect for him. What I didn't know was that he had broken a spoke in his wheel and that he was happy just to follow. I had never beaten De Vlaeminck in a sprint in my life. He finished second and I finished third.' And Danguillaume's final gesture: 'The hotel restaurant had a very well-stocked aquarium. We didn't have to go far for lobster. I put my 1000 francs (£135) of prize money from third place on the table, and we consoled ourselves.'

But let's rewind one season to discuss Merckx's third and final world title, in 1974. The Belgian team's stay in Montreal started badly. Lodged in an uncomfortable student accommodation, the team moved to the only available hotel they could find: a seedy motel.

On Sunday 25 August on the Mount Royal circuit, which has 21 climbs, Bernard Thévenet, riding solo with a three-minute lead for 115km, dreamed of becoming world champion – until just 5km from the finish line. Less than half a lap: that's all he missed out by. Would he have managed to hold on to a lead of a handful of seconds if Poulidor and Martinez – who were in the counter-attack alongside Merckx, Santambrogio and Van Springel – had protected him better? Thévenet's 'no' is categorical: 'I was done. I had no more strength. I didn't fuel up properly – and you can't get away with that.' Merckx had the good grace to admit: 'Without Van Springel, I never could have closed a three-minute gap. This title belongs to him.' Re-watching the INA footage, you can't help but feel that at least some of the rainbow jersey also belongs to the Italian Santambrogio, a former teammate of Merckx at Molteni. Poulidor, in second, and Martinez, in third, helped soften the blow for the French.

On 25 October 1972, at the Agustín Melgar Olympic velodrome in Mexico,
Merckx sets a new Hour Record by covering a distance of 49.431 km

49.431KM:
THE HOUR RECORD

'Eddy Merckx is like a metro ticket inspector. He makes small holes everywhere with a drill, even at the risk of breaking his bike frame. He does the same on his chainring. It looks like Swiss cheese.'

ROBERT CHAPATTE, A FORMER CYCLING
PROFESSIONAL AND TELEVISION JOURNALIST

On 25 October, 1972 at the Mexico City velodrome at an altitude of 2250m, Eddy Merckx set a new hour record. He covered a distance of 49.431km, improving on the previous record held by Danish rider Ole Ritter by 778m. (Ritter's record was 48.653km, set on 10 October, 1968 in Mexico City). He surpassed his compatriot Ferdinand Bracke's attempt (48.093km, 10 October, 1967 in Rome) by more than 1km. Merckx's record of 49.431km would stand for 12 years before it was broken by Francesco Moser (51.515km, 23 January, 1984 in Mexico). Moser achieved it on a futuristic bike that the International Cycling Union later deemed non-compliant, as the Italian's hi-tech machine deviated too much from the required standards.

Conversely, in the tradition of Fausto Coppi, Jacques Anquetil, Ercole Baldini, Roger Rivière or Ferdinand Bracke and Ole Ritter – those who preceded him in the record books – Eddy Merckx always knew he would go for the hour record on a regular bicycle. The Italian manufacturer Ernesto Colnago gave him an exact replica of his road bike, which is displayed today at the metro station named after Merckx in Brussels. Frame angle, fork tilt, seat post, stem shape – everything was exactly the same to the millimetre. Only the ultra-light 28-spoke wheels, fitted with very thin 95g silk tubular tyres, were different. The fixed gear has 14 teeth, with a 52-tooth chainring at the front. Each pedal stroke covered 7.93m.

The back problems of the four-time Tour de France winner had been well known for a long time. Everyone had seen him take his own spanner from his jersey pocket during a race to adjust his seat post while riding. He also had a reputation for being an expert mechanic, conducting his own tests to lighten his frames and assess their rigidity. He had about 50 in his workshop and would take 10 or so on the Grand Tours. Robert Chapatte, a former professional who entered the Tour de France five times before he became a television journalist, found it amusing. In the daily newspaper *L'Aurore*, he said: 'Eddy Merckx is like a metro ticket inspector. He makes small holes everywhere with a drill, even at the risk of breaking his bike frame. He does the same on his chainring. It looks like Swiss cheese.'

The 1972 season, his second in the Molteni jersey, was coming to an end and it had been a rich harvest: a Giro–Tour de France double, the Milan–San Remo, Liège–Bastogne–Liège, Giro di Lombardia, as well as the Omloop

Het Volk and the Flèche Wallonne. It was one of his most successful seasons since he burst on to the scene eight years earlier. The win/race ratio was phenomenal: 50/129 – a little more than one victory every three days.

It became increasingly clear that he wanted to attack the hour record, to follow in the footsteps of Coppi and Anquetil. On 31 August, after a victory in a *kermesse* in Rummen, he told journalist Willem Van Wijnendaele: 'I've got plenty in reserve after finishing the Giro and the Tour. I feel great and my legs are good. I believe I'm ready.' That is the character of a true great – having the constant need to prove themselves, always, everywhere. Always higher, always stronger. And although Eddy Merckx loved an impossible challenge, he went to Mexico City, at altitude, where the oxygen in the air is thinner and so reduces the resistance coefficient by about one-fifth.

He knew that this race against the clock would unfold before the eyes of the whole world, and not just the cycling community, which would await the outcome with fevered anticipation. Merckx was an established champion, but failure could undermine his legacy. After a season spent on planes and trains, with hours in cars (and the occasional morsel of good food, because he loved fine dining), moving from one country to another, from a Classic to a Grand Tour, from a *kermesse* to a criterium, the risk of taking on one challenge too many was very much present.

The adaptation to altitude was the other unknown variable – and it was a big one. Merckx's compatriot Ferdinand Bracke, the 1967 record-maker in Rome (48.093km/h), learned the hard way. Former Belgian champion Pino Cerami, who coached Bracke, described the two-time world pursuit champion as having 'silk ankles' – so fluid was his pedalling style. Cerami said, 'On the straights he was a world champion – no one could touch him.' Yet Bracke was to experience resounding failure in Mexico City. Here's what he said: 'Of all the hour record holders, I'm the one who turned my legs the most. My flexibility on a fixed gear was my best asset. When I decided to go for the record again in 1969, I had just become world pursuit champion for the second time, and in the Six Days I was part of the inner circle. Taking the record back from Ritter was certainly something I was capable of. So I tried Mexico City. I went there – just as I had to Rome – with zero preparation. But once I was there, even after two weeks I'd hit a wall after 10km. My lips went blue. I couldn't breathe. I did two trial runs and both were the same. At the 12th kilometre, I had no oxygen. The French riders Daniel Rebillard (1968 Olympic pursuit champion on that same track) and Bernard Darmet were there at the same time as me. They had a go at the hour record for amateurs. They failed for the same reason I did. I still sometimes think about it now, 50 years later. I regret that I did not get better support from Peugeot, my employer at the time. With a dedicated programme and specialised support I could have succeeded, but for them cycling was just a sideline. Most of the budget went into their F1 projects and rally raids. After winning the Vuelta a España in 1971, my monthly salary was 3500 francs (£465). In 1978, when I was no longer so good and whisky brand Old Lord's Splendour was my (last) sponsor, I tripled my salary just doing *kermesses* and the Six Days.'

In his preparation for altitude Merckx did not make the same mistake. It was optimal. Throughout October he followed a programme devised by Professor Petit of the University of Liège. Thirty bottles of oxygen were delivered to him, specially matched to the air in Mexico City. Six times a day, wearing a breathing mask connected to the oxygen tanks, he would get on a turbo trainer, pedal for 30 minutes and perform a one-minute sprint every five. Every day a cardiologist monitored the curve of his heart rate. After tests conducted on the track of the Gent velodrome, the newspaper *Het Volk* published the following data: 'In the course of the trial Merckx was equipped with a telecardiogram that allowed the specialist on the sidelines to track the changes in his heart rate. At 55km/h his heart rate did not exceed 140 beats per minute.' Other tests conducted by Professor Ceretelli of the University of Milan highlighted his enormous respiratory capacity: in a regular person, it's 4.5 litres; for Coppi it reached 6.8 litres; for Merckx the volume was 8.1 litres. This was combined with his incredible ability to instantly eliminate the lactic acid produced by muscle cells in a simultaneous organic reaction. Hence his exceptional ability to prolong intense effort. His legs are also excellent. Throughout that October – within a four-day span – he claimed victory in the Tour of Lombardy (though he would later be disqualified after a positive doping test) and the Trofeo Baracchi, a 100km time trial, paired with Roger Swerts.

Everything seemed to have fallen into place for him to be crowned a new conquistador in Mexico City, driven by this unshakeable motto: 'I will go. I will see. I will conquer', most commonly known as *Veni vidi vici*. The Belgian delegation landed on Saturday 21 October in Benito-Juarez, Mexico City's international airport. The record attempt was to take place on Wednesday 25th at 8.45 a.m. In the meantime, Merckx noted that the wind started picking up around 10 a.m. and that the morning dew made the track slippery. Tuesday 24th: rain. Training on the Olympic track was cancelled. He went for a long ride in the autodrome, behind the motorcycle driven by his great friend and confidante, Guillaume Michiels – known as 'The Tomb'.

On the 25th, once the track was dry he set out to try and beat the 20km record. 'If I'm feeling good, I'll keep going.' He kept on racking up the laps. At the 30km mark he said to Giorgio Albani, his *directeur sportif*, 'I'm dead.' Albani laughed: 'I've never seen a dead man going 55km/h!' In a crude, ill-fitting outfit Merckx was feeling the pain where it hurt most: the saddle. His injury would take months to heal. Each curve of the track squeezed his bloodstream tighter, the centrifugal force working against him. He lost ground. The 50km/h barrier remained unbroken but he was the new hour record holder. 'It was the longest hour of my life. But one that shimmered with stars.' After Coppi, Anquetil, Baldini – legendary giants from another era – history could not have offered a more majestic symbol.

Roger De Vlaeminck (L) and Eddy Merckx (R) in 1972

Bernard Hinault (L) and Eddy Merckx (R), five
Tours de France each, great friends after having been rivals,
reminisce about good times during the 2010 Tour de France

OPPONENTS

Whereas up until Merckx there had been a balance between the different world of sprinters, *rouleurs* and Grand Tour riders, from then onwards it was everything Merckx, everywhere. Throughout the 1970s no one escaped Eddy Merckx, and because he left an indelible mark on his era it can also be said that he mattered to those who didn't like him. What follows is a series of portraits of some of his 'intimate enemies' – sometimes winners, often vanquished. They were the cornerstone of my investigation. Their stories, told 50 years on, shine with a new light, a new tone, forgotten detail, but still emotion. They show just how different cycling was in the 1970s, which can truly be called a miraculous decade.

In the 'Grand Tour' category, Bernard Thévenet, Felice Gimondi, Luis Ocaña, Lucien Van Impe, José Manuel Fuente, Herman Van Springel and Ferdinand Bracke do not appear as they are covered elsewhere. Nor do Gianni Motta, Roger Rosiers, André Dierickx, Francesco Moser and Cyrille Guimard feature among the 'Classics men' for the same reason. At various different levels they all won epic skirmishes and are very much a part of the history of cycling. Without them Merckx would not really have been completely Merckx.

Roger De Vlaeminck

A Monuments specialist nicknamed 'The Gypsy'. One of only three riders to win all five Monuments, he won the Paris–Roubaix a record four times, earning him another nickname, 'Monsieur Paris–Roubaix'. He raced 1969–1984.

'I am the only one Merckx asked to let him win.'

One Monday in March, 2024: in Kaprijke, in the Eeklo municipality of Belgium, spring is gently emerging. Roger De Vlaeminck's house is here, situated amid rich farmlands in a part of East Flanders. It is at the end of Heinestraat, a seemingly endless road which stretches off towards a horizon of hills and meadows. He said 1 p.m. for our meeting, 'because I'm going for a ride in the morning.' He is rooted in his unchanging world. Since he turned his back on road cycling and cyclo-cross in 1988 at the age of 41 he has never stopped riding. With a 20-year career and 11 Monuments under his belt, 'The Gypsy' – a nickname he earned due to his mother's Roma heritage – was always considered one of Eddy Merckx's most persistent adversaries. With a wry smile – keen on precision – he says: 'I beat him more than anyone else and that's a source of pride. I was a fan of Rik Van Looy and that gave me another reason to want to beat him. Eventually, everyone who went up against Merckx had to give up. Apart from us. My brother Erik and me.'

He's still in his cycling gear – black jacket, black and yellow bib shorts – and apologises for being late. He shares details about his average speed for the day (23.2km/h), and slips into the dry clothes laid out near the stove. That his French is lacking in syntax is of little importance. What matters is the emotion. And the fact you are chatting to a legend – a demi-god in Flanders – who gives you a coffee, 'with sugar?' and then offers you another one makes for a strong, emotional moment. It was a straightforward exchange. 'I was the first to win four Paris–Roubaix. I don't know that there's been fiercer competition since. There were 10 or more of us who could win any Classic, each more ferocious than the other.' The most important thing in the profession? 'Having strong nerves and character.' His were forged in steel. He steps away from cycling for a moment to give an example: 'To start with I played football – I was a left-winger at FC Eeklo Meetjesland in the third division. I had a reasonable education. I was 16 years old; everyone said I was gifted and could make a career of it. One day, after a big match against Saint-Niklaas, Dr Léon, the president, came into the changing room to hand out match bonuses to the players. When he got to me, he didn't even look at me. So I said to him: 'Take a good look, because this is the last time you'll ever see me.' And I crossed over to cycling, like Erik. He was two years older than me and already doing well.'

His jaw has filled out a bit but he still stands tall, lean, clean shaven. He's up at seven. His life is rich in victories that could be mapped like a chart, with points and coloured roads marking his 259 victories on the road. In 1968, news of the potential of this future star reached the ears of Eddy Merckx, the leader of the new Faema team. The young De Vlaeminck, 21 years old, was in the process of winning the Amateur Tour of Belgium when a team attendant warned him that he was about to have a visitor: 'I saw Merckx and his guys coming back from training. It wasn't a long conversation. Merckx asked me, "Do you want to ride for me next year?" I replied politely, "Not only will I not ride for you, but I'll be riding against you."'

It was the beginning of a long rivalry that 'The Gypsy' describes as 'relentless but respectful. There was never any nastiness, even if we occasionally clashed. In fact, at first we didn't even talk to each other.' His first professional race was in 1969, a stunning victory at Het Volk, ahead of all the big names: Merckx, Sercu, Leman, Rosiers, Van Springel, Verbeeck and so on. 'The day before, I was still competing in a cyclo-cross race in Vera de la Bidasoa, in the Basque Country.' He won his first Monument the very next season with Liège–Bastogne–Liège, a race whose fairness Merckx long questioned because of the incident in the Rocourt tunnel before entering the velodrome. Of his three Milan–San Remo wins (1973, 1978, 1979), it was without a doubt the first that is the best for De Vlaeminck: 'The day before, Giorgio Perfetti, boss of Brooklyn, my new team, made us visit his chewing gum factory. In the car park there was a Caribbean blue Ferrari. I walked around it, gently running my hands over the bodywork. The boss, who called me Ruggero, said, 'You like it? It's yours if you win the Milan–San Remo tomorrow.' That Monday morning I was at the wheel of the blue Ferrari. I didn't even have the papers for it, I was in such a hurry.'

With his unusually long arms he fiddles with his phone, scrolls through photos while talking. Then he zooms in on one and asks: 'You know him?' With thick, black hair, a cherubic face and a hint of mischief in his eyes, it is his great friend Jean-Pierre Monseré – known as 'Jempi', – who died during a race almost right in front of him. It was a tragedy for Belgium. A sudden deep dive into the memory: 'With him life was a great laugh. Ah, the pranks we pulled together...' The silence that follows seems endless. He starts the conversation again: 'Do you know how many kilometres I rode three days before *De Ronde* or the Paris–Roubaix to be sure I was ready for the fight?' Without waiting for an answer: 'Three days before I'd force myself to do 380km. To the 260km of Gent–Wevelgem I'd add 120km behind a motorbike.' Like Rik Van Looy and Eddy Merckx, 'The Gypsy' won all five Monuments on the calendar and had a particular preference for Paris–Roubaix, 'especially when Merckx finished second behind me.'

In the official record books of the Classics, the name Roger De Vlaeminck is inextricably linked with the Paris–Roubaix: he had four victories, four second-place finishes, one third place, and only a single puncture in 14 outings, over which he covered a total of 3700km of worn-out roads and cobblestones. Behind this detail lies the obsessive care he took in fine-tuning his inner tubes and his Clément silk tyres – 26mm wide for the front wheel to better absorb the shocks. They spent several years drying in the dark before being glued and inflated – not too much – with helium because it's lighter. They were ready to go in the 'Hell of the North', as the race is sometimes known. With his torso horizontal, shoulders steady, elbows square and wrists bent, he was a picture of perfection on pedals. He had a divine intuition for the terrain, a reptile-like fluidity. It was attributed to his 'tightrope-walking' skills from when he was a teenager, when he'd carefully steer his bike between chairs and tables before riding down stairs without touching the ground to finish his act. Sometimes, to win bets, he'd slot his wheels in tram tracks, going from one bistro to another, and the rounds of drinks would pour in. On those infamous cobblestones of the Hell of the North, he exuded such charm and elegance you would have thought he'd just stepped out of an Yves Saint Laurent, Dior or Balenciaga fashion show. In the style of Céline (similar to the Irish writer James Joyce), but more rock and roll, Philippe Bordas, in his sublime book *Forcenés*[30] saw him as a 'Keith Richards with calves, playing with his back to the crowd and who didn't care.' And further on, regarding his gear: 'The Gypsy used the first five cogs, never the last one; Keith did the same, getting rid of that fucking sixth string.' His knack of spotting hidden traps under deceptive puddles and picking the best line on the cobblestones came from his extensive cyclo-cross training. 'There's no better training than cyclo-cross for developing reflexes, balance, skill and sustained extreme effort. I won 112 out of 180 over my career, including two World Championship titles – amateur and professional.'

Eddy Merckx was never able to win his fourth Paris–Roubaix, but De Vlaeminck knows that the comparisons stop there: 'A three-week Grand Tour was too much for me and Merckx was too superior. I don't think we'll ever see the likes of him again. He was 10 times stronger than the second best. By contrast, in an eight-day stage race I was very much at ease and I could compete with anyone,

---

[30]Literally, 'madmen'.

even the great Merckx. I proved that by winning Tirreno-Adriatico six times and the Tour de Suisse once.' He comes alive with a sparkle in his eye: 'That 1975 Tour de Suisse – you won't believe me – but it is my best memory. Better than the Paris–Roubaix, Milan–San Remo and all the others. On that last day I beat Merckx three times: at the sprint in the demi-étape in the morning, in the afternoon time trial and at the finale, where he finished in second – 1 minute behind.'

The two men buried their differences and have been more appreciative of each for a long time now. De Vlaeminck can't resist revealing something else: 'That year in Switzerland I had won absolutely everything since the start. Eddy came to see me on the second-to-last day and said, "Roger, you could let me win one," and we finished first and second in the order he wanted.' I don't know if people can truly grasp the significance of that gesture today: 'I'm the only person Merckx ever asked to let him win. I did it wholeheartedly and without hesitation, but I could have said no. Because two years earlier in the final of the Trofeo Laigueglia – it was team Brooklyn's debut in the peloton – the boss came up to me and said: "Ask Merckx if you can win. It would be a good advert to get things started." I asked Eddy, who said, "Oh, come on!" On the finish line: Merckx first, De Vlaeminck second.'

To truly show the bonds of friendship that now tie these two immense champions, he came out with another curious anecdote: 'Still on the 1975 Tour de Suisse, we were both at an anti-doping control. I went first and I was waiting for him, to go back to the hotel. After a while, Eddy said, "I can't go, I can't do it. Have you got any left?"

I waited until the doctor was busy and I peed for Eddy. What would you call that? For me, it was the most beautiful bond of trust.'

By the end of 1977, Merckx had begun his descent toward the end of his career. Before the start of a criterium in France, the five-time Tour winner, looking worried, approached De Vlaeminck: 'Say, Roger, you're not going to drop me at the first corner are you?' The Gypsy replied: 'Eddy, you are Mr Merckx, you have nothing to worry about. And he stayed on my wheel.'

Ten years later, when the cycling demons pulled De Vlaeminck out of retirement for an extra two-year stint in cyclo-cross, the only one who believed in him, providing financial backing and equipment, was none other than Eddy Merckx. Nobody needed to ask why, when his son was born, 'The Gypsy' chose the name 'Eddi' (ending with a vowel rather than a consonant – 'to make it a bit different'). He plays football, just like his father in the early days.

De Vlaeminck is a great man and a timeless free spirit from a bygone era of champions. If I had a crown, I would have placed it on his head. As he showed us to the door, amid the leaping and barking of Bats and Vina, his two border collies, 'Mr Paris–Roubaix' whispered into the ear of Robert Janssens, the man who serves as my interpreter: 'You know, Robert, it is an honour for me to have spent my career with a journalist like you.'

Merckx and Freddy Maertens at the Championship of Zürich in 1975. Behind the duo, Francesco Moser grimaces

Freddy Maertens

Two-time world champion (1976, 1981) and Vuelta a
España winner in 1977. He raced 1971–1987.

'Montjuïc 1973 had a terrible consequence for me: I was
angry with Merckx for 30 years. In 2004, at a meeting of
former riders in Beaujolais, we sat down and talked things
through face to face. It took hours, but we made peace
with each other. We promised we'd never talk about it
again in public.'

Between Eddy the elder and Freddy, his junior by seven
years – nearly a generation apart – lies a long history of
champions, ambition, rivalry and historic clashes. Merckx
had already won four Tours de France, three Giros and
the five Monuments when Maertens emerged on the
scene as a pro in 1973. Bursting on to the scene would be
more accurate, for the young man from Nieuwpoort –
massive, broad-shouldered, strong-thighed – tasted glory
with his very first Tour of Flanders in his debut year.
Freddy Maertens was good at everything and possessed a
breathtaking turn of speed. Over 100m he could go from
60 to 75km/h. Yet he never won a single Monument in
his career, whereas Merckx had 19. Maertens was actually
a far tougher opponent than that simple statistic would
suggest. His 233 victories make him a legend: 2 World
Championships, a Vuelta a España, 35 stage victories in
Grand Tours, 3 green jerseys, a flash of yellow in the Tour
(9 days), some rose in the Giro (5 days), the Grand Prix
of Nations, Paris–Tours, and plenty of podiums – it all
adds up. A rock-solid career.

The story of this prodigy has been told a hundred times and is often romanticised. Towards the end, where the misery of shaky social class, insurmountable money problems, alcohol and depression intertwine, it reads like a misery memoir. But the fallen champion, who put on 20 kilos, weathered everything the storm could throw at him, unlike his friend and teammate Marc Demeyer, winner of Paris–Roubaix 1976, who eventually hanged himself. Freddy stayed the course because he had a guardian angel as the troubles piled up: Carine, his wife, his soul, his anchor, his rock. She saved him from his ills, helped to restore his honour and his dignity. There's an immense tenderness between these two beings who have supported and stood by each other for 50 years.

In Bertem–Rumbeke, West Flanders, their latest house looks out on to a small country road. Under the force of the north wind, poplars bow, rain threatens and summer is late. Repeatedly postponed, my meeting with the man who was, for Merckx, an irrepressible, unbreakable and tenacious rival for five seasons – from 1973 to 1977 – was utterly essential. The handshake is straightforward, the 'Angel' smiles warmly. Sitting with his back to a portrait of him in the rainbow jersey, painted by the Spanish artist Miguel Soro, Maertens gets straight to the point: 'Merckx? The greatest I ever knew, the greatest of all. There was no one like him. With him, the tactics were simple: stay on his wheel, otherwise you'd be in trouble.'

However, at birth, nature had not been kind to the son of Simone and Gilbert. During his first year he could hardly eat anything. He was getting weaker and there seemed to be no medical solution. Months of anguish, fever. 'Until the day someone told my parents about a miraculous spring near Furnes. My father brought back jerrycans full of it for my baby bottles and then for cooking my food. From that point on all my problems evaporated and a new life began.' A gift from the gods, Maertens? Fate hasn't been unkind. In May, 1979, unable to hold his handlebars because of a serious elbow problem that no one could fix, he went to meet a specialist in Philadelphia. The DC10 took the journey Amsterdam–New York–Chicago. During the flight, Maertens pointed out to his doctor that an 'engine on the wing was making a funny noise.' Landing in NY, Maertens and the doctor continued their journey and the DC10 left for Chicago. It exploded on take-off. The death toll was 271.

It's clear from his physique that Maertens was a tough, strong rider who would have had no trouble holding his own on the cobblestones. That skill, that strength, goes way back. Raised the hard way by his father, at the age of 13 he was a newspaper delivery boy, hauling 20, sometimes 30 kilos of magazines and papers on his bike rack. During the season he would cycle for hours in the sand, delivering to the campsites along the coast. In the afternoon, it was time for training. His road training partner was called Michel Pollentier. The two were inseparable. His father monitored everything. At 16, Freddy had to be home by 8 p.m. or he would be punished. No dating allowed. 'One day he caught me holding hands with a girl, and in a fit of rage he sawed through the frame of my bicycle.' He was racking up the wins. 'I owe a large part of it to Louis Bouvé, the man on the motorcycle, my faithful coach. He was always on time whatever the weather. On occasion he was so affected by the cold that he couldn't even get off his bike.'

The rest of the story unfolds with Guillaume Driessens – known as 'Lomme' – his *directeur sportif* at Flandria. He was a controversial, wily, opportunistic and outspoken character – and Merckx couldn't stand him. Maertens affirms, 'Yes, but he was crafty and a good strategist. Demeyer's victory in the 1976 Paris–Roubaix was down to him. Only one car was following the breakaway: his. He blocked all other *directeurs sportifs*. I had fallen and was already in hospital when he went up to Moser, De Vlaeminck and Kuiper and loudly shouted to Demeyer, "Take it easy, Marc! Maertens is on his way back. He's 30 seconds behind." And for 40km, Demeyer just coasted along in the shelter of the slipstream.'

But ghosts haunt his memories, too; that of Paul Claeys, the boss of Flandria, haunted him for a long time. 'He made me ride all the time. One year I was up to 210 race days. He was a tyrant with the riders. The night of my victory at the 1976 Grand Prix des Nations in Angers, he made me ride all night so I would be at the start of a *kermesse* in Oostrozebeke the next day at 11 a.m. Another time, he made me ride with a fractured arm, which didn't stop me from winning. My father ran a Flandria bike shop, so as far as he was concerned we were indebted. Flandria was the biggest mistake of my career. It was my father's shop against my signature, even though I had a contract ready in Italy with Scic for almost double the money.' Inner torment and the prevailing blues of the 1970s echo in his voice.

And life continues in his memories. The passion for racing, where riders came to 'arrangements' (he doesn't deny it) was always strong. At the Tour of Lombardy in 1974, in the final stretch he was out in front in a breakaway. But, feeling an urgent need to eat to ward off a bonk, he dropped back to his team car for provisions. Briek Schotte was driving: 'Give me a feed bag!' But Schotte had been hungry and had eaten everything. They caught me. Unable to pursue, I had to give up.'

Liège–Bastogne–Liège, 1976: 'In the final, Bruyère, one of Merckx's teammates and Van Springel, who wore the Flandria jersey like me, were in the breakaway. I was less than a minute behind. I know I'm going to win unless something happens. Van Springel can't go for it – he's my teammate – and I was going to close the gap. But what I didn't know was that Van Springel had sold out to Bruyère and was taking all his relays at full speed. I finished just a length behind Bruyère.'

Tour of Flanders, 1977 in Koppenberg: bike changes were allowed. 'I took a new bike 20m before the designated line and got disqualified. But at the same time I was in a break-away with De Vlaeminck, who told me he hadn't won yet that season and would I be willing, for 300,000 Belgian francs (£6515) ... I shook on that one. I could see he didn't have the legs, so if I didn't get going, it was over; we'd be caught. So I rode as if for myself. Flat out for 80km, and he won. We met again some time later and he gave me 150,000 Belgian francs (£3258), which I split three ways with Pollentier and Demeyer. He said, "The rest will come later, I'm not flush right now." Almost a year went by and nothing. So one day I went to find him and he just said to me, "What are you talking about? We never mentioned money." De Vlaeminck could be like that. A really great rider, but a very small man.'

His World Championship jerseys from 1976 and 1981 still carry the scent of sweat, struggle and anxiety – even more so the ones that slipped through his fingers, in 1973 and 1974. Deeply moved, he confides: 'Montjuïc 1973 had a terrible consequence for me – I was angry with Merckx for 30 years. In 2004, at a meeting of old riders, organised by Paulo Cinquin in Beaujolais, we sat down and had it out face to face. It took hours, but we made peace and promised never to talk about it again in public.'

In Montreal in 1974, a prime example of the dirtiest aspects of cycling perhaps shook him even more: 'During the race, my *soigneur*, Jeff D'Hondt, left the stand to pick up a sandwich. In his absence, another Belgian *soigneur*, Gus Naessens, took the opportunity to put drops of something into my bottle. I drank it when D'Hondt passed it over to me. Ten minutes later, I had to stop on the side of the road; everything was coming out at both ends. I could barely stand. I had to drop out. Years later, Naessens was about to sign a contract with Flandria. I looked him square in the face and said to him: "Rumour says it was you in Montreal. Before you sign, I want you to tell me the truth. Did you put drops in my bottle or not?" He confessed everything. I'm human and I'm kind; he was down and out and needed work, so I let it slide.'

Ostuni 1976 brings a smile back to his face. 'We hardly spoke to each other, but when Merckx gave his word he meant it, and he worked for me so I could win.' He cannot hold back a sneaky smile: 'It was just the two of us and Moser in the final, and I knew he'd negotiate because he had no chance in the sprint. "Nine million for you if I win!" I saved him money.'

Jan Janssen

Janssen's major wins include the 1968 Tour de France, the 1967 Vuelta a España, the 1964 World Championship and the 1967 Paris–Roubaix. He raced 1962–1972.

'I was his opponent; he took me for his enemy.'

Oosthoevestraat in Kapellen is a leafy street which is notable because it borders Belgium and the Netherlands. On the north side the houses are Dutch, on the south side they are Belgian. Jan Janssen, winner of Paris–Roubaix and the Vuelta a España in 1967 and the Tour de France in 1968 was Dutch, but settled at number 157 – in Belgium. His teammates and neighbours Erik Breukink (former yellow jersey bearer on the 1989 Tour) and Adrie van der Poel (winner of the 1986 Tour of Flanders, the Liège–Bastogne–Liège in 1988, and father of Mathieu), live on the other side of the street. A pro cyclist from 1962 to 1972, Jan Janssen frequently competed against Eddy Merckx, about whom he admits, while swearing under his breath, 'Shit yes, he made me suffer on a bike all right, but who didn't struggle against him?' And without further ado: 'Eddy and I have never been great friends. I was his opponent; he took me for his enemy. He always had a problem with Dutch riders.'

What they did have in common was being world champions in the same year – 1964, in Sallanches. Eddy with the amateurs, Jan with the professionals, but that's about it. Everything else is along the lines of the famous Gainsbourg/Birkin song: '*Je t'aime, moi non plus*' ('I love you, neither do I'). For example: 'I can't deny it, Merckx was a truly great champion, the greatest of his time – but he had the best riders working for him in his team. Bruyère, Van Den Bossche and Huysmans were often stronger than he was. And as far as I know, they weren't well paid.' Another example: 'Have you ever seen him laugh on a podium? I never have. I'll buy a round for anyone who shows me a photo of that.'

A 1980s soundtrack plays in the background and suits the atmosphere perfectly. While Jan Janssen hands out espressos to his friends – Bennie Ceulen, another former pro, and Pascal Sergent, historian of the Paris–Roubaix – French-Italian singer Richard Cocciante croons about feeling lovestruck in 'Coup de Soleil' (Sunstroke). And, during the break, while there is a casual mention of a '15-kilo carp that lives at the bottom of the pond, which you can see over there by the bay window, next to the camellia', the French-Canadian singer Robert Charlebois promises he'll 'return to Montreal to marry the winter.'

From his years at Pelforth-Sauvage-Lejeune (1962) and Bic (1963–1968), Janssen's got plenty of good stories: 'I shared Jacques Anquetil's philosophy of cycling; he loved good food and champagne. He loved life. It didn't stop him from winning five Tours de France. Sometimes, right in the middle of the season we'd get really drunk. We were adversaries and accomplices at the same time.' 'The ultimate happiness' for Janssen, is 'to have met wonderful people, some of whom became my best friends. With Roger Rosiers, who, like me, often had to fend for himself in the Classics, including his Paris–Roubaix in 1971 – that's something that has lasted 50 years.' And bringing up the end of his career: 'When Flandria pushed me out in 1972 – forgetting to pay me – I was worn to the bone, squeezed out like a lemon. I usually went straight to bed after a stage. We rode constantly from February to October and after a season on the road I went straight into the Six Days. One year I did more than 180 race days.'

Jan Janssen juggles his 12 seasons of memories until suddenly it escalates, and, remembering Paris–Roubaix in 1967, it gets intense. It was nearly 60 years ago, but for him, that year's winner, it will always be yesterday. With a nod towards the cobblestone trophy, the symbol of his victory, here's what remains in his memory: 'There were about 10 of us going for the win as we entered Roubaix. No one had the strength left to attack. We all knew it was going to come down to a sprint. Up there was Van Looy, Altig, Willy Planckaert, Sels, Motta, De Cabooter, Poulidor and Merckx. When we got on to the track I had a shock: my rear tyre was going down. It was a simple calculation: if I went up the bank, I risked losing the tyre off the rim – I had to hug the inside line. I can't remember any more if it was me or Altig who went first, but the sprint started from a distance and I won without a problem. It was the most beautiful sprint of my whole career. Van Looy was second. Merckx eased up and finished 50m behind.' End of part one.

Part two unfolds at one of those reunions of former cyclists where real life is merely a backdrop, as they're so busy unpacking their little bags of memories. This one's all Paris–Roubaix: weather, tumbles and punctures fill the conversation. We're back to re-living the final straight in 1967. Everyone agreed that Janssen was the strongest that day, and as he shared his thoughts, he suddenly turned to

Merckx and delivered a biting remark – one that would not be soon forgotten: 'Why are you talking about the sprint, Eddy? That day you weren't even in the picture.' But Merckx was no slouch at this game either – he, too, could be caustic. The old riders met up again. Round after round of beer. Jan no longer knows if he's had five or six. He'd had enough and just wanted to go home. Eddy shouted over, 'Come on, Jan, another!' 'No, I'm OK. I'm done.' 'Oh – I can see why you only won one Tour de France.'

The 1964 world champion's strong character did not earn him only friends. The 1968 Tour de France was the last to be run by national teams and Merckx did not take part. Janssen had to wait until the final individual time trial stage to dethrone Herman Van Springel and pull on the yellow jersey. He only got to wear it twice: on the final podium in 1968 and one other time in the 1966 Tour. To achieve this, he claims to have fought on two fronts: 'My adversaries and my own *directeur sportif*, Kees Pellenaars, who continually undermined me. In an interview with *Vrij Nederland*, three days before Paris, he said, "If Jan Janssen wins this Tour, my mother-in-law could win it too." War was declared. Pellenaars – God rest his soul – was the Dutch De Muer: highly influential and only out for himself. The difference was that De Muer owed me a lot of money. I never saw a penny of it.'

In the same vein, Janssen's frankness and temperament could work against him in the cycling world, where he was seen as an anti-Merckx plotter: 'I just said out loud what most riders were thinking. They feared reprisals but I didn't, and one day in the press I called for a revolt.

Why not band together? That's the only way we'll be able to deal with him. No one took any notice, and in Belgium I became the least popular rider to the extent that people hurled insults and threats.' Merckx's suspension, which was lifted despite his positive doping control in Savona during the 1969 Giro, only fuelled his anger: 'I still maintain that there was a double standard. Eddy tests positive and it goes all the way up to the King of Belgium. And, as if by chance, they find a procedural error that means he's there at the start of the Tour de France. The same year, in Paris–Nice, I refused to pee for the doping control because Dr Bouteille was ogling us all – and I got suspended for four weeks. Did I get a hearing in front of Queen Juliana?'

The two champions met again at the start of the 1969 Tour in Roubaix, heading to Belgium, then the Netherlands. In Woluwe-Saint-Pierre – Merckx's hometown – Janssen received a truly detestable welcome. But he made amends when the Tour headed towards Maastricht: 'I went to see Merckx, who was wearing the yellow jersey after Faema's success in the team time trial and I said to him, "I'm not interested in the general classification, but I'd really like to win the stage that finishes in my home town." Eddy's reply was, "OK, sure. No problem." I attacked 5km from the finish, gained 100m, turned around and what did I see? Van Den Bossche and Steven flat out in pursuit. I sat up.' Jan Janssen arrived in Paris 52 minutes and 56 seconds behind Eddy Merckx. In the Bible it is forbidden to yoke an ox and a horse to the same plough. With those two there was no risk of that verse being contradicted.

Walter Godefroot

'The Bulldog of Flanders' won four out of five Monuments and achieved 61 professional victories. He raced 1965–1979.

> 'You couldn't have gone out cycling in that weather. Suddenly we saw a man on a bike riding along in the distance. He was dressed like a fisherman with a poncho, shoe covers and gloves. It was Merckx.'

In 1970, pre-season training camps had long been a mandatory ritual. Everybody did them. As the seasons changed, trends shifted, but Italy was always a popular choice. After Sicily, the Riviera and Lake Garda became the go-to spot. Many Italian teams chose to prepare in Manerbe, which was known for its mild climate and the surrounding terrain. Walter Godefroot, who already had an impressive list of victories – Belgian Champion in 1965, Liège–Bastogne–Liège in 1967, Tour of Flanders in 1968 and Paris–Roubaix in 1969 – was now sporting the Salvarani team jersey for the first time. Felice Gimondi was following the advice of his friend and teammate Giancarlo Ferretti, who was stunned by 'the work rate of the little guy with the big legs.' The offer couldn't have come at a better time. Godefroot had been labelled a 'tourist' by his former boss at Flandria after the 1969 Tour of Flanders, which was won by Eddy Merckx.

Manerbe, January, 1970: on the shores of Lake Garda the Salvarani riders were sharing the same hotel with the Scic and Dreher teams. Eddy Merckx and his Faemino team were in a hotel nearby, and the Molteni team with Marino

Basso and the Filotex team with Franco Bitossi were not much further away. Every evening they exchanged information or spied on each other. One morning it was absolutely chucking it down – a real deluge. It wasn't fit for a dog, let alone a rider to be out. This anecdote, often recounted by Walter Godefroot, surprised everyone but him: 'We were watching the rain come down through the large bay windows. The road was empty. We were loafing about, hanging around in the comfy chairs, shoes in hand, ready to leave, but it was still coming down hard. You couldn't have gone out cycling in that weather. Suddenly we saw a man on a bike riding along in the distance. He was dressed like a fisherman with a poncho, shoe covers and gloves. It was Merckx. He was out on his ride, totally oblivious to the storm. His determination always gave him a head start.'

Godefroot and Merckx turned professional in the same year, 1965. The former started at the Four Days of Dunkirk, the latter at the Flèche Wallonne. Three months later at the Belgian Championship in Vilvoorde, Walter – who was built for sprinting with thighs like tree trunks (he could snap his bike chain when he set off) – won ahead of Eddy. 'I don't think I ever beat him in a sprint finish for the win,' Merckx admitted. Godefroot, who was one of very few who could compete with him in the Classics, points out that 'it didn't happen often, but it did happen once, in 1973, at the finish of Liège–Bastogne–Liège on the track at Rocourt.' The podium of *La Doyenne* was as follows: 1: Merckx. 2: Verbeeck. 3: Godefroot. They were each very different in terms of character as well as background. Merckx, from a modest but comfortable background, benefited from excellent training conditions. Godefroot was working class, with poor parents. He had to take his bicycle on the train to travel to races, surrounded by his own supporters. In the *kermesses*, where he found himself with Rik Van Steenbergen and Rik Van Looy, he was so shy and intimidated 'that I didn't know if I should call them "Rik" or "Mr".' The only thing they had in common – he and Merckx – was the unwavering desire to win. It was amplified in Merckx, determined in Godefroot, 'except that I didn't want to win everything all the time; that wasn't my character.'

Occasionally their rivalry took a bad turn. In 1966 at the finish of the Dwars door Vlaanderen (Across Flanders), Merckx crowded him against a barrier, causing him to fall. He was disqualified. 'What made me angry,' Godefroot recounts, 'is that the next day the press referred to the collision as a work accident.' His anger was turned up a notch in 1967 at the finish of Liège–Bastogne–Liège, where the sprint went in his favour: 'The journalists wrote a big article about Eddy, who didn't even know about the change in the finish line due to the snow, and a tiny piece about me who had actually won *La Doyenne*.'[31] Even more significantly, regarding his non-selection for the World Championships that same year in Heerlen, a substantiated rumour said that it was Merckx who was behind it. Thousands of supporters demonstrated for Godefroot at a criterium in Drongen. The Royal Belgian Cycling League didn't budge and the World Championship departed without him. For a very long time he held Merckx responsible. Today, he is of the

[31] *Dans l'Ombre d'Eddy Merckx* (In the Shadow of Eddy Merckx), 2012, Johny Vansevenant

opposite opinion: 'Merckx assured me and I don't doubt his word.'

Before burying the hatchet at a criterium in France in 1970, they went up against each other in a few major confrontations. Tour of Flanders, 1968: on one side Godefroot, Van Looy and Sels; on the other, Merckx and Reybrouck. Van Looy, Merckx's sworn enemy, was in the lead group, which worked to Godefroot's advantage. He beat Reybrouck by two lengths in the sprint at Meerbeke. 'I soon learned that although it was good to have friends in the pack, it was better not to have enemies.'[32] Paris–Roubaix, 1969: Godefroot arrived at the velodrome by himself. Merckx, second by 2 minutes and 39 seconds, complained of gastric problems the whole race. 'When asked, I say jokingly I only won the Paris–Roubaix because Merckx was ill!'

But there has always been respect between the two. Merckx said that he was impressed by Godefroot's dedication to Gimondi in the 1970 Giro. Godefroot raises his hand, affirming he 'always competed fairly against the one who pushed me to be my best. I would not have forgiven myself if I'd been the reason Eddy lost a race.' It was Merckx who made the first move after a criterium. It was much like what would happen between him and Ocaña on the eve of a memorable À travers Lausanne race, where the hatchet was finally buried following a long night and several bottles of whisky. The version attributed to Merckx, during and after that famous post-Tour criterium in 1970 – this time without whisky – is as follows: 'Hey, Walter, are

[32] *Eddy Merckx: La Biographie* (Eddy Merckx: The Biography), 2015, Johny Vansevenant

we going to hold a grudge forever? Why don't you come and ride for my team?'

The offer remained on the table for a long time but was never taken up. Godefroot would later admit it was the biggest mistake of his career. Instead he joined Peugeot, saying that he 'met champions and good people', but also experienced his worst memory in a Tour de France. 'In 1971, in the Orcières stage I had two punctures and the car of *directeur sportif* Gaston Plaud – meant to be my support – was nowhere to be seen. On arrival I lost out by two seconds. The next day in the Marseille stage about 15 riders – including the entire Kas team – came in outside the time limit but they were all allowed to continue. Maybe I was too much of a threat for Guimard; I was only 3 points off his green jersey. But if that's not a double standard, I don't know what is.'[33]

And although Merckx and Godefroot both started their professional careers in 1965, Walter had one more year in the sport before he bowed out in 1979. He paid this tribute as an epilogue: 'It makes sense that you decline when you reach the end of your career. But when it came to character, even at the end Merckx was still unbeatable. That last victory of his in the 1976 Milan–San Remo? Only he could have done that.'

[33] *Dans l'Ombre d'Eddy Merckx* (In the Shadow of Eddy Merckx), 2012, Johny Vansevenant

Frans Verbeeck

'The Milkman' is known for his many podium finishes in the Monuments without ever winning one. He raced 1963–1977.

> 'My first Omloop Het Volk, in 1970, sums up my entire life. I was up at five in the morning to deliver milk, butter and fresh cream to bakeries... I ate two ham sandwiches at the wheel... I led the whole race from the front... In the sprint Rosiers and Dierickx had no chance.'

How many times, since I started this account of the Merckx years, did I hear this: 'You can be a great cyclist, a champion, without being an excellent racer. But only by winning a Monument can a cyclist truly enter the pantheon of greats.' This thesis is wrong. Frans Verbeeck never won one of the five Monuments on the calendar, but he is a monumental rider. Between 1970 and 1977, he was on the podium in 8 of the 42 Monuments he contested. If you broadened that field to the Classics during the same period, he made it to the top ten 56 times. If he hadn't already been saddled with a series of unusual nicknames, his adversaries could have given him another: 'The Workhorse'. But as it turned out, Frans Verbeeck was first called 'Soupe' (Soup), but later came to be known as 'The Milkman of Wilsele'.

One Saturday in June 2023 in Wezemaal, in Flemish Brabant, north of Leuven: Verbeeck made his fortune there, but not in a dairy. That was before, in another life. He reoriented his career into sportswear, in partnership with his son Marc. Together they founded Vermarc – the first syllable of

Verbeeck combined with his son's first name. Today, their business is number one in Belgium – ahead of all international equipment suppliers – and they supply clothing to half of the professional cycling peloton, football teams and the French-speaking Belgian athletics league. In a somewhat solemn tone, he points out: 'Merckx was a great rider and he was truly a gentleman. When I started my business, he put me in touch with all his contacts. When you come recommended by Merckx everything is simpler. He gave me his stamp of approval.' It leads perfectly to his next point. Though wrinkles now line his face and his muscles are smaller, you can still make out the rider he once was – the one who relentlessly faced up to Merckx – by his broad shoulders, massive torso and working man's hands. It's a mixture of strength, courage and resistance. In just a few seconds, the romance of a bygone era comes flooding back. His father worked down the mines. His mother made and sold soup. The Verbeeck family valued hard work above all else. At the age of 14 and without a licence, the young Frans delivered 500-litre vats of vegetable soup by van. He and his mother sold it in the village square of Overijse to grape pickers harvesting the region's best-known varieties: Léopold III, Ribier and Muscat. That's where his first nickname, 'Soup', came from.

But let's skip ahead to 1963, when young Verbeeck, then in the 'independents' category, landed his first professional contract with the Kint-Réno team: 'I signed for 2500 Belgian francs (£53) per month. I was paid over 10 months. It was a pittance, but I had to eat. I raced whenever I could, and in 1964 I was offered a place at Wiel's Groene Leeuw, on world champion Benoni Beheyt's team.' Then everything happened almost too quickly: 'I was mainly taking part in *kermesses*. One day in Heusden, mid-race, the mechanic got me off my bike and told me: "I just had a call from Albert (De Kimpe, the *directeur sportif*). Go home and pack, you need to be in Rennes tomorrow, starting the Tour de France." I lasted nine stages in that 1964 Tour and finished in the top 10 three times before I had to drop out.'

Verbeeck finished second in the Frankfurt Grand Prix the following year, but when he added up his earnings at the end of the month there was barely enough to cover little Marc's baby bottles. It was a simple calculation: he hung up his bike and bought a dairy. It was another life. Up at 4 a.m. Load the cart with milk churns, packets of butter, cream, then off on the delivery route. 'The Milkman of Wilsele' – named after his village – was born. But the cycling demon still possessed him, and he would sometimes sneak his bike into the van and go for a ride. His thing was the fixed gear. He came across a cobbled climb that looked like a wall, near Kessel. It had sand on the sides, grass in the middle and large cobblestones all the way along it. 'The first time I couldn't even make it to the top. Halfway up, I just fell off into the sand. I also had a circuit around a lake where I'd ride 100km. I came home exhausted. I ended up confessing everything to my wife, who did not want me to take up riding again. When I did get back into racing with smaller teams like Okay-Whisky and then Watneys, I felt a bit lost. To be safe, I kept on delivering milk in the mornings and training in the afternoons. I remember on 1 January, 1969 I went to the Kesselberg and climbed it 40 times in a row on a 52 x 16 fixed gear.'

His tales bring a sense of wonder over those old races, but they're the real deal – no messing around. From that world of the past, from his passion for racing – still intact and deeply ingrained within – he confesses that he has 'lived a dream life. Belonging to that generation of riders is a privilege like nothing else. It is a gift from above, although I did a lot more than just pray to get it. When you get up at four in the morning to deliver milk, then ride a bike for another three hours – sometimes more in the afternoons – to the point where you can't even walk when you get off, if someone had called me crazy, I would have said yes, for sure. Some days, when Angèle, my wife, did the milk round for me, I'd cycle all the way to the Ardennes. It was a round trip of 380km.' He rarely got the better of Merckx – 'he was simply too strong for us' – but there were also times when 'I was pedalling through treacle.'

'The Milkman' won the Amstel Gold Race (1971), the Het Volk circuit (1970, 1972) and became champion of Belgium in 1973, beating Merckx in a sprint. He enjoys telling the story: 'Eddy had broken away and was alone up front. Godefroot, De Vlaeminck and then Van Springel tried to catch him, but they all got stuck on the steepest part. When I attacked I knew I would catch him. The circuit was just like my training route and I knew it by heart. And of course, when it was just me and him, he asked me to take a turn at the front – but I refused. It was just like what he had done in Gent–Wevelgem a few weeks earlier, where he had stayed on my wheel in the finale to beat me in the sprint. The chasing group in that title race included Willy Planckaert, who was not only the quickest, but also someone Merckx had a rivalry with. He kept pushing the pace and I became champion of Belgium.'

He still sighs with disappointment when he thinks back
to Liège–Bastogne–Liège in 1973, where he, Merckx and
about 10 others arrived together at the Rocourt velodrome: 'The finish line had been moved. I won the sprint
on the wrong line; Merckx beat me by 3cm in the photo
finish on the right one. I had insomnia and nightmares
for ages afterwards.' Nevertheless, the impressive record of
'The Milkman' speaks for itself. He finished second two
times in the Tour of Flanders; in 1974 he beat Merckx, but
was outdone by Dutchman Cees Bal; in 1975 he stayed
with Merckx for over 100km through the hills before
finally cracking in the finale, utterly spent. However, it's
not that fantastic Flanders epic, still fresh in the memory,
nor his Belgian champion's jersey that he brings up when
choosing the race that meant the most to him in his career.
'If I had to name one,' he says with a smile, 'it would be
my first Omloop Het Volk in 1970. I won it again in 1972,
but that first one sums up my whole life. I was still doing
both jobs. I was up at five in the morning to deliver milk,
butter and fresh cream to the bakeries. On the way back,
I got into my old Volkswagen – one of the old ones with
indicators that stuck out of the sides – and I drove to Gent.
I ate two ham sandwiches while I drove and put two more
sandwiches in my jersey pocket. I arrived three-quarters
of an hour before the start. I had this incredible strength
in me. I stayed at the front for the whole race. I was in
the right breakaway, while Merckx and De Vlaeminck got
caught. At the sprint, Rosiers and Dierickx had no chance.
That day, my life turned around. My contract was increased
from 3,000 to 15,000 Belgian francs (£325) a month.' Who
could deny such a man a place in the Hall of Fame?

Eric Leman

'The Butcher' was well known for winning the Tour of Flanders three times. He raced 1967–1977.

'Merckx never gave you a choice.'

Eric Leman is one of those riders specialists call a 'true, true *Flandrien*' – a hunter in the Classics, ready to make any sacrifice to win what is, for a *flahute* (Flemish tough guy), the most beautiful race in the world: the Tour of Flanders.

They form a caste, a not-so-secret society, proud of their exploits. Leman achieved the feat three times: in 1970, 1972 and 1973. He shares this distinction with Achiel Buysse and Fiorenzo Magni who did it before him, and Johan Museeuw, Tom Boonen, Fabian Cancellara and Mathieu van der Poel who accomplished it after him. These three victories are further elevated by the presence of Eddy Merckx, the 'god of gods', in the final showdown - three landmark dates that Leman proudly printed on his business cards. Although he proclaimed himself the 'fastest rider in the world' during the first half of the 1970s ('my opponents fought to get on my wheel') it should not be taken as arrogance, but rather as great self-confidence and towering ambition. The great Briek Schotte, nicknamed 'Last of the Flandriens' (two-time world champion and two-time Tour of Flanders winner), had a sharp eye for spotting someone with 'the right fibre, passion, the talent.' He became his first *directeur sportif*. Schotte didn't mess around when he recruited Leman to Flandria in 1968. Although Leman complains it was 'only a tiny contract', Schotte was clearly making a big move. 'This guy has the character and legs of Van Looy.'

The butcher's apprentice (Leman's first trade) from Izegem would prove him right. 'You had to really want it, and my brother Robert, who had tried cycling as an amateur, pushed me to become what he couldn't. My day at the abattoir started at 6 a.m. At noon, I was out making deliveries, and only after that, at around 5 p.m., would I leave to train. Nothing could have distracted me from that burning desire to become a professional. Well, maybe hunting, my great passion,' says Leman with a laugh. Selected for the Belgian B team to take part in the Tour de France in 1968, he won the 21st stage – with a sprint, of course. By the end of the following season, significant tensions had arisen between Walter Godefroot and him. It was a question of supremacy. Godefroot, who had already claimed Liège–Bastogne–Liège in 1967, the Tour of Flanders in 1968 and Paris–Roubaix in 1969, issued an ultimatum. It boiled down to 'either he goes or I do'. Leman provides the explanation: 'Imagine it like two predators and only one prey. I would never have given up my share and nor would he. A true *Flandrien* is like that: obstinate, tough in the face of pain. They never complain. They don't feel the cold. I never wore gloves to race, except in Paris–Roubaix because of the vibrations and blisters. So, Walter left to ride in Italy.'

In 1970, the rivalry between them over the past two seasons was at its climax, 'not to mention that we could all be demolished by Merckx, who wanted to win everything. I never doubted my legs. I had what was called double acceleration. It was my speciality. At full speed, I could give a burst of power that shot me forward and meant I could beat my rivals.' With three wins in *De Ronde*, Leman is particularly proud of beating Eddy Merckx three times. But it was the first, in 1970, that has a special place for him: 'In the finale, Merckx and Godefroot teamed up to take me down. Walter attacked first, gaining 250m, and I chased. Merckx was on my wheel, refusing to take the relay. It took me 2km to catch him. I knew Merckx would counter immediately. Fortunately, I had some in reserve, and I followed him with no problem. At the sprint, they both knew they would lose.' He told of his great joy to Dries de Zaeytijd, the driving force behind the KOERS Museum of Cycle Racing in Roeselare: 'There were no showers at the finish line; it was a free-for-all. I got on my bike and went into the countryside on small roads. I had never found it so beautiful. I drove up to a farm I didn't know. I didn't tell them that I had just won *De Ronde*. I asked the farmer's wife if I could clean off the mud. She put some hot water in a basin and I started washing while I replayed the best moments of the day in my head.'

In March 1971, Leman was devastated by the news of the death of Jean-Pierre Monseré, a very close friend. That evening the Flandria team abandoned the Paris–Nice. There is a saying that goes, 'If you close one door to misfortune it will sneak in through another.' And 10 days later an unlikely drama struck again. Returning from the Amstel Gold Race, Eric Leman was driving home with his wife, Marie-Rose, and his sister when they suddenly found themselves in a patch of heavy fog. He violently went into the back of the vehicle in front of him, driven by Roger De Vlaeminck. His wife went through the windscreen and died shortly afterwards. He was devastated. It took all of Briek Schotte's persuasive powers to help him overcome the intensity of that nightmare and push him to start the Tour of Flanders just one week later. He finished 24th over the finish line in Meerbeke. Cycling became his lifeline. In the Tour de France, Leman won three stages. Impressed by his strength of character, courage and dedication to the profession, Maurice De Muer offered him the chance to start over with the Bic team. He joined Roger Rosiers, his compatriot who had just won Paris–Roubaix, and Luis Ocaña. But he did not find it easy to fit in. Roland Berland, a former teammate, remembers him as 'a distant guy who kept to himself, didn't make the effort to speak French and was rather introverted – unlike Rosiers, who was Flemish to the bone – outgoing and happy just to be there.'

Leman rightly points out that he was not adequately supported in his preparation for the Classics: 'When training, we'd leave for a 200km ride, but at the first drop of rain, off they went! The French would turn around and go back. Only the Tour counted for them, and July was five months away. So I continued alone. I suffered, but I actually liked it – hurting myself. Until I couldn't walk when I got off the bike. I had no choice if I wanted to lead. Merckx never gave you a choice.'

His teammate Christian Palka secured his selection for the 1972 Tour of Flanders at a *kermesse*, some three days before the start. He says, 'Those dizzying, roller-coaster-like roads, studded with cobblestones, attracted all the strongest riders for a final practice. De Vlaeminck, Verbeeck, Rosiers, Leman – all the *flahutes* were there. During the race, I was at the front, and naturally, I put myself to work for the 'big guy' – that's what I called Leman, because he was a bit hefty in the rear. After the finish, he congratulated me. In the evening, De Muer called on the phone. "I hear you're riding well at the moment. (Silence). Well, if you feel like you're ready, you can do the Tour of Flanders on Sunday." I figured out that Leman and Rosiers had given him the message. They did a good job. At the Deerlijk feed zone, after Courtrai, they were going full pelt. The Old Kwaremont was 10km away and I was at the front of the pack, Leman beside me. At the top I was almost on Merckx's wheel. Just behind me were Rosiers and Leman. I made it over all the climbs – not as many as there are today – right next to Leman, and on the downhill I'd given him the push he needed to get back on. My legs gave out a bit on the Bosberg, but the hard work was done. It came down to seven riders, and Leman just dominated the sprint, pushing Merckx to seventh. On Monday morning, in *La Voix des Sports*, journalist René Deruyk wrote that I had "earned my stripes as a great *domestique*".'

Leman completed his hat-trick in 1973, winning for Peugeot at the expense of Maertens and Merckx. Past his peak, 'The Butcher' no longer boasted about his powerful 'engine' – his biggest strength – but rather lamented his ever-longer recovery time. 'It took me two weeks to get back to normal sleep after a season of 150 race days. When I felt my body was weakening I didn't try to fool myself. There was no point in pushing on. You try harder, but you're just getting slower anyway. So I thought about hunting trips. I didn't want to give them up, and I was right.'

Rik Van Looy

Two-time World Championship winner and the first cyclist to win all five Monuments, 'The Emperor' raced 1953–1970.

'His name is both a legend and a brand. He was also an advertisement, because Willem II, the cigar manufacturer and his new sponsor from 1967, started producing Van Looy bands, featuring his effigy on the best Havanas in their range.'

Belgium, which never had an emperor, found one in Herentals – Rik Van Looy, also known as 'Rik II', because in the dynasty of Riks, Van Steenbergen preceded him. In 1965 Van Looy won everything there was to win in terms of Monuments and Classics. His dominance was so complete that he didn't so much have a team at his service, more an 'Imperial Guard'. He was 32 years old and in his 13th season when he claimed his third Paris–Roubaix win. Though he had already tasted immense success he was driven to keep winning – to become the Minotaur who dominated every corner of his competitive labyrinth.

His beginnings are so distant that his first professional pedal strokes in 1953 are from the time of Fausto Coppi, Gino Bartali, Fiorenzo Magni, Louison Bobet, Ferdi Kubler, Hugo Koblet, Rik Van Steenbergen, Stan Ockers, Briek Schotte, Jean Brankart and many others. After that, Van Looy reigned over his contemporaries: Jean Fortier, André Darrigade, Jean Stablinski, Fred de Bruyne, Noël Foré, Gilbert Desmet, Peter Post, Nino Defilippis and Miguel Poblet. In 1965 he was nearing his record for victories: 371. A trophy list? More like an empire! Two World Championship titles, three Paris–Roubaix, two Tours of Flanders, one Liège–Bastogne–Liège, one Giro di Lombardia, multiple Gent–Wevelgems, Paris–Tours, Paris–Brussels and one Flèche Wallonne plus 37 stage wins in the Grand Tours. When a new, third generation of riders stormed in at the start of the 1965 season, their hunger for glory and control was entirely to be expected.

'Emperor Rik' did not know – or perhaps chose not to acknowledge – that the wheel of time was spinning at a crazy speed. How could he have known it, when, in the evenings, his teammates hung on his every word, laughed when he laughed and marvelled at his stories they all knew by heart? And if, perchance, anyone failed to toe the line they were out immediately – just like Eddy Merckx, who, despite being the reigning amateur world champion in 1964, refused to show any deference. When he joined Solo-Superia in 1965, Merckx arrived with a clear vision, ready to redefine the cycling world on his own terms. He was only 22, eager to forge his own path and live with no regrets. He saw cycling as a path to freedom, not servitude. With his good friend Patrick Sercu, the 1963 world sprint champion and 1964 Olympic kilometre champion – and also his new Solo-Superia teammate – they often discussed it and made plans. The pair had already made a decent reputation for themselves in the Six Days. Merckx knew right away that he would never be part of the Van Looy clan: 'At the Paris–Luxembourg they treated me like a nobody.' Jan Buggenhout, his manager, nonetheless believed he was doing the right thing by offering him a spot on the team with Van Looy and Van Steenbergen, two experienced riders; he thought that a hostile environment was a good opportunity for a young rider. He was wrong. Merckx became the team's scapegoat. There was sarcasm and mockery at the dinner table. As well as jibes about his clothes and his physique, he was laughed at for the food his mother, Jenny, made for him. The 'Emperor of Herentals' gave him a nickname: 'Jack Palance' after the American actor who was known for his prominently bowed legs, like Merckx's, and for playing villains who were 'a bit slow-witted'. It was more than just joshing, it was bullying.

The shy, respectful Merckx, who drew much strength from his family ties, suffered greatly from this humiliating and crude treatment. Practical jokes followed the insults. His front wheel was unscrewed before a training ride, his saddle smeared with grease or glue. They even messed with his tyres in the hope that he'd crash. The young Merckx, 12 years younger than 'the Emperor', was in dire need of a change of scenery. In 1966 he joined the Peugeot team, where Tom Simpson – whose impressive résumé included the Tour of Flanders, Milan–San Remo, the Tour of Lombardy and a World Championship – didn't hesitate to play a few tricks on him, with the complicity of Van Looy himself.

It took significant strength of character to dare to stand up to 'the Emperor'. Because even though he was advancing in years, even though he was no longer the superstar, he was still an authority. He was even – dare I say it – a living legend. Van Looy's name held such capital that it transcended the man himself. His name became both a legend and a brand. A legend, because even at 37, a train-load of fans would follow him to watch him race abroad.

He was also an advertisement, because Willem II, the cigar manufacturer and his new sponsor from 1967, created Van Looy bands, featuring his effigy on the best Havanas in their range. Unchecked ego? Without a doubt. Guaranteed success, too. Who would have thought this adored and respected legendary champion – winner of all the Classics – would stoop so low as to be part of such personal attacks on Eddy Merckx? To give you an idea of Rik Van Looy's immense stature and popularity, even at the end of his career, his supporters in Campine and throughout the rest of Belgium still numbered in the tens of thousands.

Merckx left in 1966 and from that point his sphere of influence grew and grew. By 1968 he had already swept up two Milan–San Remos and a Paris–Roubaix, and he led the national team as the reigning champion at the World Championships in Imola. Van Looy, on the other hand, barely made the cut. Merckx didn't object. On the big day, the team left Van Looy behind at the hotel, and by the time 'Rik II' had made his way to the starting point, the race had already started without him. It was not a disaster, and he caught up with the peloton fairly easily. The incident was dismissed as a simple mishap – though not by him. He never forgave the crime of lèse-majesté, and to this day he remains convinced it was a plot against him.

In 1969 he started his last Tour de France. He was approaching 37 years of age. Right from the first stage the Faema team took control and dominated. Julien Stevens, a teammate of Merckx, wore the yellow jersey. At the start of the fourth stage, from Charleville-Mézières to Nancy, Van Looy tried a daring bluff and attacked solo. Immediately, three Faema riders gave chase. With a single gesture, Merckx stopped the pursuit. And so, it was with his great rival's blessing that Van Looy claimed his seventh stage victory in the Tour de France. Two days later, exhausted, he arrived too late at the Ballon d'Alsace and surrendered his number 99 bib. The truce between the 1969 Tour winner and his famous elder lasted barely 100km – just one stage in Eastern France. In the post-Tour criteriums across France and the local *kermesses* in Belgium, the knives were out again. Knowing a thing or two about strategy, Van Looy simply latched on to his young rival's wheel and stayed there. The 1969 Tour winner stopped pedalling. The two adversaries freewheeled along, locked in a stand-off, allowing the pack to pass them. The bizarre antics made them a laughing stock. The same thing happened in Liedekerke, Rijmenam and Hasselt, where an exasperated Eddy called Rik a 'stubborn old goat'.

But time heals all wounds, and Merckx stepped up to fund and help out with the cycling school Van Looy later established. But half a century on, the old wounds are still raw and a debate on Belgian channel BRT, with Van Steenbergen present, almost blew up into a storm. Van Looy did not appreciate being called a 'wheel-sucker' live on air, but he did save face with this remark: 'Eddy is still the best rider of all time. I have only one regret, that I did not get to compete with him in my best years. I think my record would have been better than his. And at the sprint, I was faster.'

Joop Zoetemelk inquires about Merckx's health during the 21st
stage of the 1975 Tour de France between Melun–Senlis. Merckx had
been suffering from a double fracture of his left jaw since his crash

Joop Zoetemelk

In 1985, at the age of 38, Zoetemelk became the oldest winner of the World Championship. He won the Tour de France in 1980 and raced 1970–1987.

'Merckx never admitted defeat; that was his strength.'

The seemingly ageless Joop Zoetemelk became world champion at the age of 38 years, 8 months and 29 days. Throughout his 18-season career, which stretched from 1970 to 1987, the Dutchman from Germigny-l'Évêque took part in 16 Tours de France and finished every single one. He reached the top of the podium in 1980 and made second place six other times. He came up squarely against Merckx at his most formidable, and then, without a break, encountered the same from Hinault. But he has no regrets: 'There's no changing history with ifs and buts,' he says, instead choosing to focus on how 'I won a big race every season.' Talking of Eddy Merckx he says bluntly: 'He wasn't my friend. He criticised my lack of aggression. He probably didn't know it, but we were completely behind him and happy to just follow. A Mini can't compete with a Ferrari. We barely said hello to one another, and the press only widened the gap between us.'

Zoetemelk had a front-row seat during the famous stage of the 1971 Tour at Orcières, where Luis Ocaña seized a decisive advantage for overall victory: 'I didn't lead for even one centimetre, I'll admit, I just couldn't do it. I wasn't having a good day. I was criticised for it, but, objectively, it was up to him to take responsibility, not to blame others – as he often did. In a race, in the Tour, you don't have friends. Sometimes you make a temporary alliance, but otherwise it is every man for himself. I don't agree with Merckx when he said that we were happy to see him suffer on the Orcières climb. And the very next stage showed how he bounced back. Merckx never admitted defeat; that was his strength. In the pursuit towards Marseille, Ocaña said, "Give him the two-minute lead; he'll burn himself out." But come Paris, Merckx was in the yellow jersey while Ocaña was out.'

Today Zoetemelk says he cannot single out The Cannibal's most impressive feat: 'It was as if what interested him more than winning was pushing his limits further and further. You never knew what he'd do next – or how he'd do it – but I thought he pushed his winning obsession too far. I didn't have that mentality. When I was beaten, if I had ridden well I was happy. Merckx, on the other hand, never accepted the idea of defeat, and he lost sleep over it more than a few times for sure.' Character and circumstance never allowed a close relationship to develop between these two great champions. 'In Belgium, I knew what was waiting for me at the start of a race. Boos and whistles. After my accident in 1974 it took me nearly two years to get back to – and maintain – a good level. From time to time, I'd win a good race – Paris–Nice in 1975, La Flèche Wallonne in 1976, and I finished second in the Tour de France that year – but I was starting to worry.' Joop remembers a road World Championship in Yvoir in particular where he was given police protection after receiving threats. 'The Belgian team were overwhelming favourites with Merckx and De Vlaeminck, but when Kuiper broke away, I made sure never to ride alone and I preferred to wait for a small group. I felt more at ease.'

Eddy Merckx was no longer in the peloton in 1980 when Joop Zoetemelk, at 34, finally rode his way on to the list of Tour de France winners. Five years later, defying his age, he clinched the World Championship in Giavera del Montello, Italy, making him the oldest rider ever to earn the rainbow jersey. Long after he'd retired, returning from a bike ride, The Cannibal couldn't have been further from his mind: 'Eddy Merckx phoned. You need to call him back.' He is still surprised: 'On the phone, he explained that he was personally organising a ride in Austria for all former world champions and that naturally he'd thought of me.' It was a gesture that really meant something to me. We had an amazing time, a long way away from the old rivalries.'

Bernard Hinault wins the first stage of 'Dauphiné Libéré'
race ahead of Merckx in 1977 at Saint-Étienne

Bernard Hinault

Five-time winner of the Tour de France who also won three Giros, two Vuelta a Españas and numerous Monuments. He raced 1975–1987.

'A very strong bond ties me to Merckx.'

Eddy Merckx once called you his successor, his spiritual son, even. How did that make you feel?

'Really proud above all. I was just getting started in professional cycling when he gave me a big helping hand in winning the Dauphiné in 1977. It was a spontaneous gesture. I'd had a nasty crash and he was irritated that the others were trying to take him out. When the greatest rider in the world waits for you and says, "get on my wheel, hold on," it is exhilarating, I felt like he genuinely wanted to help me. It was an extraordinary motivation for me. Without him I wouldn't have made it. Through me, he got his revenge for the hard time they'd given him. "Merckx, Hinault's teammate" – it still makes me smile every time I think about it.'

A few weeks prior he was in the finale of your first victory at Liège–Bastogne–Liège. But he was no longer the great Merckx...

'Whoa, whoa, careful now, you had to be there. The race had been very tough; 20 riders classified. There were six of us in the breakaway; I countered Dierickx's attack and beat him in the sprint. Behind us, only by a few seconds, Eddy was sixth.

Funny thing is that he was still there with me in the finale in 1980. He had stopped riding in 1978, but he was in the race car behind me. And from that dreadful Liège–Bastogne–Liège, two things stick in my mind: the freezing weather, snow all day and the presence of Merckx. Being watched by someone who achieved such extraordinary feats in their career gives you the strength to rise to the occasion.'

There are five Tours de France each on your records, but no Tour together. The year he retired, 1978, you won your first. You couldn't ask for a better handover of power.

'It's certainly a telling coincidence. Circumstances and fate took their course. Perhaps there was a little more to it than luck. A very strong link ties me to Merckx, still. I think it was a good handover.'

Did you have the same racing style?

'The same desire to win, yes. But my riding style was different. Eddy went all in. He raced the entire calendar: the Tours, the Classics, criteriums, the Six Days. Non-stop from 1 January to 31 December. It was simply phenomenal. I focused more on specific goals, but you've got to remember that racing was done all year round in those days.'

When you were young, was Merckx a source of inspiration?

'I had two idols who truly inspired me and nurtured my progress: Jacques Anquetil and Eddy Merckx. I took what I needed from each one.'

What was your very first impression of Merckx?

'It must have been on a Paris–Nice, in 1975. Zoetemelk won it and Eddy must have been second. I remember people kept telling me, "Did you see? Merckx is here. It's going to be tough." I remember saying to a journalist, "Merckx has two arms, two legs and a head. Same as me. He wants to win and so do I." The message was clear. It was my debut, I wanted to fight, I wanted to ride, and Merckx was part of that motivation. I never started a race saying, "Uh-oh, this guy or that guy is in it." If you think like that you may as well go fishing.'

First World Championship in 1976, in Ostuni. In the sprint Merckx came fifth and you came sixth. Another sign?

'Finishing on Merckx's wheel was simply the outcome of the race – no more, no less. Talking about how I finished sixth in a World Championship on Merckx's wheel is of no interest to me. Ostuni, for me, is a bad memory. I had a real chance to be world champion but it didn't work out because of internal issues within the French team. When you ask someone to close a small gap, and I mean a small one, and the guy says he can't but then a moment later he attacks knowing he's not up to it – how do you think you're going to bring home the jersey? [Silence]. I don't want to name names. It was a long time ago...'

In your era – Merckx's era – you were riding full seasons and typically finished with an average of 130 to 150 race days. Today, with a few exceptions, riders target specific goals, clearly separating the Grand Tours from the Classics. Could you have ridden like that?

'Someone who loves competition can't race that way. Cycling is a game, it's a passion, but above all, it's not just a job. Anyone who approaches it as just a job is wrong. They're missing out on something essential: the pleasure of it. I often tell myself I did really well to enjoy it. I also say to myself – thinking about those who race 50 days a year – how they must be so bored, spending their lives waiting.'

Who do you feel closest to, Anquetil or Merckx?

'I think I am closer to Eddy. I think I'm more like him. In the saddle we loved to win a Classic with a special performance – as well as the Grand Tours, of course. We think the world of each other.'

Mark Cavendish in the rainbow jersey is congratulated by Merckx.
The sprinter from the Isle of Man's top speed allowed him to beat his illustrious
predecessor in the number of stage wins in the Tour de France: 35 against 34

TEAMMATES

'We made our way through sheer hard work.
But everything has a price.'

PATRICK SERCU, FRIEND AND
TEAMMATE OF MERCKX

Between his debut in 1965 and his final season in 1978 – in
which he only raced five days – Eddy Merckx enjoyed the
company of 130 teammates. From a simple *domestique* at
Solo-Superia and Peugeot to becoming the team leader at
Faema from 1968, he strived to give the word 'teammate'
a familial connotation. 'Because,' says Merckx, 'it's within a
family that you learn to become a man.' Some dedicated
their entire careers to him: Joseph Bruyère, Frans Mintjens,
Joseph Spruyt and Victor Van Schil rode by his side for nine
seasons. Jos De Schoenmaecker, Jos Huysmans and Roger
Swerts re-signed eight times. Ward Janssens took part in all
his campaigns for six years, Martin Van Den Bossche for five
and Ludo Delcroix, Patrick Sercu and Julien Stevens for
four. As in any family, there were squabbles and petty jeal-
ousies, but his sporting achievements and personal impact
speak volumes after 14 seasons. Eleven, if you exclude
his early days at Solo-Superia, where Rik Van Looy, who
reigned supreme, gave him such a hard time; and his experience at Peugeot, where at 21 he had little say against

the old guard such as Tom Simpson, Roger Pingeon and Ferdinand Bracke, all of whom were set in their ways and privileges.

In fact, it all began in 1968. Merckx was only 22 when he took charge at Faema and immediately demonstrated undeniable authority. He confidently led experienced riders like Vittorio Adorni, who had already won the Giro. Adorni belonged to the Italian clan that was imposed on him by the sponsor; he would only stay for a single year. His chosen men knew why they were there: to ride for him with no questions asked. To be enlisted under the Merckx banner meant giving up all personal ambition, pushing oneself to the absolute limit in the pursuit of a yellow, pink or rainbow jersey and numerous Monuments. It was an adaptation of Alexander Dumas's motto of the three Musketeers: 'One for all and all for one.' As the sole leader Eddy Merckx understood the value of their efforts and always repaid that dedication. In the 1975 Tour, he was second overall when he suffered a fall in Valloire at the start of the 17th stage. Despite a fractured jaw and sinus, he refused to give up so his teammates would not lose out on their share of his winnings. Of the 1,113,505 Belgian francs (£24,170) earned by the Molteni team on arrival in Paris, half went to Merckx, because of his two stage victories and his second-place finishes in the general classification, points and King of the Mountains categories.

There is no monument to immortalise the acts of bravery by Merckx's men. The life they loved no longer exists. All that remains are old newspaper cuttings, emotions and memories built on their powerful pedalling on the flats, in the mountains – where no one could surpass them and where everyone – even Merckx – was pushed to the limit. Those victories belong to them, too. In another team some of the generals could have aimed for a share of power, targeted a Monument, a King of the Mountains, a green jersey or stage victories. For Merckx's men the leader's word was law. Italo Zilioli, who spent only one season riding for Faemino, wiped away a tear when we met as he relived memories from 55 years ago. 'Faemino? *La piu bella di tutti*.'[34] He was captivated by the team's 'organisation, discipline and prevailing spirit.' He felt it was 'like a monastic order where only the leader mattered.'

Merckx had a magical hold over his teammates. It was undoubtedly the primary reason for the success of the Merckx empire. How else do you explain it? Let's pause for a moment to consider the example of Joseph Bruyère, a formidable rider, an essential link in the chain, who had two Liège–Bastogne–Liège wins and three Het Volk titles to his name, not to mention the yellow jersey in the 1974 and 1978 Tours. The man from Walloon had only one flaw, and he acknowledges it himself: 'To lead you need mental strength, nerve and the ability to make decisions. But I had self-doubt and I couldn't handle the pressure.' But his first Liège–Bastogne–Liège in 1976 – with a 100km breakaway alongside Van Springel – was more than worthy of the great Merckx. And when he took the lead of the peloton, the boss himself sometimes had to intervene: 'Easy, Joseph! Easy.' Regardless, the man from Liège, very much the Belgian's standard bearer, was an 'unconditional Merckxist, and happy to be the unsung hero.'

[34]'The most beautiful of all'

Victor Van Schil, a former diamond cutter, was already 29 when he joined Faema in 1968. Merckx, who initially took him for an old lag, quickly changed his mind. In the mountains his pace invariably spelled trouble for the opposition. Winner of La Flèche Brabançonne in 1968, fifth in the Paris–Roubaix that was won by Merckx the same year, and then second in a memorable Liège–Bastogne–Liège in 1969 alongside his leader, the rider from Antwerp made loyalty a rule of life. When he ended his career at the age of 37, 'Vic' – who passed away in 2009 – had completed 21 Grand Tours (11 Tours de France, six Giro d'Italia, four Vuelta a España). That detail is important; and Merckx greatly appreciated his Campine mentality (down to earth, pragmatic). He found those from the Campine region (known as Kempen in Dutch) to be reliable, good-natured individuals who never complained – and formed the very foundation upon which he built his successful squads.

Like Van Schil, Frans Mintjens was from that same region, and along with Jos Spruyt, Jos De Schoenmaecker, Jos Huysmans and later Roger Rosiers they formed what Belgian journalists referred to as the 'Campine Connection'.

In the 1970 Tour of Flanders, Mintjens was in a breakaway with Tony Houbrechts, but he held back from taking his turns at the front because 'the boss was never far behind', and 'big races were for big riders'. However, on that day, Merckx did not catch up and Mintjens's sacrifice only earned him a fifth-place finish. Mintjens was an 'always-on' rider – ready at any time. 'Frans didn't wait for the TV cameras to be rolling to take his turns,' stated Bob Lelangue, his *directeur sportif*, while praising his 'honesty and bravery'. You can add his bluntness to that.

Mintjens couldn't stand it when some in the team were hiding: 'Two days before a time trial, Swerts would save his energy, and we had to pick up his share of the work. Since he performed well and gave his all, he'd spend the next two days recovering and his work would fall on us again. I never accepted that.' Sought after by the biggest teams who offered to triple or even quintuple his salary, Mintjens only ever knew one leader throughout his entire career. 'What I admired most about Merckx was his stoicism. I saw him nervous, sometimes stressed and worried, but I never heard him complain. During the 1974 Tour his shorts were full of blood every day at the finish, because of a saddle injury. He won that Tour with an eight-minute lead.'

A rider in the true Campine tradition, Jos Huysmans was considered one of the most talented. With strong tactical sense and cunning, he could do everything: ride hard on the flat, climb and sprint. But what Merckx most valued in him was his ability to lead sprints; when he took the front with 3km to go, no one could get past him.

Huysmans was already 29 years old when he put on the Faemino jersey in 1970, and had a decent list of placings: fifth in the Paris–Roubaix and Liège–Bastogne–Liège in 1965, fifth in the Paris–Roubaix again and ninth in *La Doyenne* in 1966, eighth in the Tour de France 1967, first in the Flèche Wallonne and second in the Amstel Gold Race in 1969. Scrupulously honest, he couldn't help but punch Jaak De Boever in the face the day after the 1968 Grand Prix E3. They had been in a breakaway together and De Boever had begged him not to drop him, promising not to contest the win. But 50km further on De Boever had forgotten everything, and easily beat him in the sprint.

Huysmans' devotion to Merckx was limitless. At his peak as a *domestique* in the mountains and on the flats during Merckx's fourth Tour de France – where he finished ninth overall – his masterpiece was undoubtedly the starring role in the long breakaway to Marseille in that 1971 Tour. Robert Bouloux, present that day, remembers him as a 'crazy guy, who was shouting, gesticulating and encouraging Merckx and Wagtmans whenever the pace dropped.' 'A solid gold teammate,' Merckx said, later making him *directeur sportif* in 1978 at the head of the C&A team. He then offered him a role as his number two in his bicycle factory. When Huysmans passed away in October 2012 after 35 years of loyal service, Merckx stated he had 'lost a brother'.

The 'Campine Commando' wouldn't be complete without Jos De Schoenmaecker, one of the best climbers of his era alongside Martin Van Den Bossche. With Merckx he played the role of the pacesetter in the mountains, where his pace wreaked havoc. One day in a mountain pass, Gimondi – utterly spent – shouted at him: 'Basta, assassino!'[35] Merckx greatly regretted his absence in the Orcières stage of the 1971 Tour, where he lost eight minutes to Ocaña. De Schoenmaecker had to watch the stage on television due to a fractured femur he sustained in the Grand Prix du Midi Libre. He was a cheerful man who loved life and enjoyed a joke. Alongside Ward Janssens he was instrumental in shifting the mindset at Molteni. 'Sometimes in the evenings at the dinner table we started singing and joking – lightening the heavy atmosphere.' That too should be credited to Merckx, who understood

[35]'Enough, assassin!'

it as a necessary release after an exhausting day and before another gruelling one. Jos stayed for eight years at Molteni, Fiat and C&A. After his cycling career, in 1983 he tragically suffered a severe industrial accident on his right hand on a metal lathe, which severed his fingers. Eddy Merckx had a special bike made for him to allow him to continue riding. All the controls were located on the left handlebar.

Ward Janssens, a former teammate of Poulidor – whom he described as a 'decent bloke' – joined Molteni in 1973. 'At first I didn't even dare speak to Eddy because he intimidated me so much.' Janssens' talent as an entertainer was on a par with his climbing ability in the saddle. 'After Huysmans, De Schoenmaecker and Van Den Bossche had done their work I would sometimes finish them off. There was a collective pride in it.' Without a single regret he, too, turned down incredible offers from Italy: 'When we were with Eddy Merckx everyone made a good living. With two Grand Tours and around 30 crits each season, there was certainly enough to keep food on the table.' When he made his career transition, his selflessness and loyalty were rewarded with a position at the Eddy Merckx bicycle manufacturing company.

Of all his 130 road companions, one holds a particularly special place in Merckx's heart: his lifelong friend Patrick Sercu. They grew up together, came up through the junior ranks and started their professional careers in the same year with the same team (Solo-Superia). Their bond was further strengthened on the track during numerous Six-Day races. They only raced for four seasons on the same team, but they had a truly deep and supportive friendship. One a climber, the other a sprinter but both from the same modest background, they were very similar and worked to defend the same values: respect, honesty, generosity. 'We made our way with hard work, by the sweat of our brow. Everything comes at a price,' said Sercu, who was often held back by what he called 'the six-hour saddle limit... Beyond that, things got tricky for me in the sprint.' About Merckx, who he knew better than anyone, he dared to say: 'He's the kind of man who doesn't function properly unless he's under pressure.' Wearing the yellow jersey and holding the green jersey during the 1974 Tour when riding for Brooklyn, it was Sercu who brought Merckx and De Vlaeminck closer together. That year journalists became suspicious of an odd alliance between the Brooklyn and Molteni teams, dubbing it 'BrookMol'.

The former Olympic champion in the kilometre (1964), world amateur sprint champion (1963) and professional sprint world champion (1967 and 1969) raced on the track until he was 40, sponsored in his last three seasons by Eddy Merckx Bikes. Patrick Sercu, born in Roulers, West Flanders, was 73 years old when he passed away in April, 2019.

At the start of the world road championship in Stuttgart in 1991,
a fan nostalgic for the Merckx years hopes for a successor to his idol

Merckx working on one of his racing bikes

'WHAT'S YOUR WATTAGE?':
MODERN CYCLING

'New bikes are so fast that a rider on the wheel
of the one in front of him hardly even has to
pedal. With this excessive pursuit of aerodynamics, we're part of Formula 1.'

JEAN-JACQUES VANDENBROUCKE, FORMER
PROFESSIONAL TEAM MECHANIC

Cycling is one of the sports that has evolved the most
over the last 30 years in terms of technology, equipment,
nutrition and strategy. For the modernists it's all about
innovation, improvement and boosting performance. But
for the purists this sophistication and radical change has
distorted the very essence of their sport. If stars of the 20th
century such as Anquetil, Van Steenbergen, Bahamontes,
Gimondi or Ocaña, alongside many others, were suddenly
propelled on to today's Tour de France, they would wonder
what planet they had landed on.

Imagine them seeing a nutritionist at a restaurant, weigh-
ing each rider's spaghetti down to the gram on digital scales.
Or encountering a 'data scientist', busy on his computer,
cross-referencing rider data including watts, calories and
blood sugar, using a power meter installed on the bike.

Or listening to a rider ask a teammate: 'How many watts do you put out in the final 500m?' Astonished, Anquetil would ask for a translation and the data scientist would respond – in 'Python language' – that watts are a central data point in output, and that it is essential to collect, sort and analyse them as part of understanding a rider's personalised ecosystem. All of this is done to better monitor the evolution of the rider's pedalling profile using diagrams, histograms, pie charts and algorithms. At the mere mention of a 'pie' chart[36], the five-time Tour winner would bounce and smile, recalling his 1964 Tour de France. At the time, on a rest day in Andorra, he proclaimed, 'Rest days are for resting, not riding.' Out of defiance, he took part in a traditional méchoui (roast lamb feast), indulging in sangria and lamb.

As they wander around, these glorious returnees then head to the hotel car park where technical assistants – formerly known as mechanics – are polishing the bikes. Jean-Jacques Vandenbroucke made an entire career of it. He only got a brief taste of professional racing, his dream fading after only a few weeks. After the sudden death of his father in 1971 he became the guardian of his brothers Jean-Luc and Jean-Paul, 13-year-old twins. Years later he re-entered the profession on the mechanical side, following in the footsteps of Jean-Luc, who was a professional cyclist from 1976 to 1988, racking up 73 victories. Even after his son Frank – the most talented rider from the Vandenbroucke family – won a monumental Liège–Bastogne–Liège in 1999 before his tragic decline and death

---

[36]camembert in French

in 2009, Jean-Jacques remained dedicated to his craft, meticulously adjusting, tuning and perfecting bikes 200 days a year.

At his home in Ploegsteert, a small Picardy Wallonia commune whose name translates to 'ploughtail' in English, the oldest of the Vandenbroucke siblings has put away his tools. He hasn't completely retired from the world of cycling, however. Cameron, Frank's daughter, has made him great-grandfather to little Jules from her relationship with the Belgian sprinter Tim Merlier. 'Without getting involved in the mechanics or his training, I follow Tim closely. When I see his all-carbon bike, with 5- to 9cm rims, 12-spoke wheels to reduce air resistance and ceramic bearings in the bottom bracket, I compare it to bikes from the 1970s, with steel tubes, flat rims, 36-spoke wheels and steel ball bearings: they weigh half as much. Six and a half kilos today, 12 kilos then. Carbon is the norm. Now everything on a bike is aerodynamic – tubes, handlebars, brake levers, pedals, seat post, electronic derailleur – and not a single cable is visible. New bikes are so fast that a rider on the wheel of the one in front of him hardly even has to pedal. With this excessive pursuit of aerodynamics, we're part of Formula 1.'

Another notable observation he doesn't fail to point out are the gear ratios: 'If we just take a look back to the early 2000s we've gone from seven to 12 speeds on the rear. Victor Campenaerts, who won the combativity award at the 2023 Tour de France, is frequently cited as a powerful rider – a 'big engine' – because he can push a 60 x 11 gear setup. Or Tiesj Benoot, a solo breakaway specialist, who uses a 54 x 10 gear ratio. They're increasingly pushing bigger gears.'

In family gatherings, Jean-Jacques Vandenbroucke can't help but smile when Tim gets out his tabletop scale at meal times: 'Data is now part of their world, just like many things we weren't allowed to do. Staying on their feet, climbing stairs and running were among the forbidden activities. Back at the hotel in the evening, if a rider wasn't lying down on their bed they'd be told off. Today, in his training programme, Tim does 30 minutes of running every week.' When it comes to the changes, what captures his attention most is, of course, the training. 'In my day, during pre-season training camps, we'd ride five or six hours, two by two. We'd rack up a huge number of kilometres. Intensity came later, in the first races. These days, races are simulated in training with high intensities dictated by software that can recreate a race situation. You can input the profile of a Tour de France stage or a mountain pass into your computer. You can even add wind and weather and ride the Ventoux in the comfort of your garage.'

This drive for performance optimisation encompasses a vast array of elements. Today's rider races little and trains a lot, often at altitude. The most popular high-altitude training spots are: Teide, a volcano in the Canary Islands (3700m); the Sierra Nevada mountain range in Granada (3400m); and Livigno in Lombardy (1800m). The goal, of course, is to multiply red blood cells, which allows riders to pedal longer without producing lactic acid, thanks to a higher percentage of red blood cells. However, these training camps, paid for by the riders themselves, are expensive – about 5000 euros (£4390) for three weeks. So, a clever inventor developed altitude tents – with a reduced oxygen level – which can be set up at home. When Sep Vanmarcke was forced to end his career in 2023, at the age of 35 due to scar tissue found on his heart muscle (putting him at risk of a cardiovascular incident), the Paris–Roubaix specialist (second in 2013, fourth in 2014, 2016 and 2019) humorously announced at the end of his press conference: 'All I have left to do is take down the altitude tent in my garden.'

This phenomenon is so widespread that in Spain, specifically on the Costa Blanca in the province of Alicante, the Syncrosfera hotel, owned by former Russian cyclist Alexander Kolobnev (bronze medal in the road race at the Beijing Olympics), has been offering training camps with altitude rooms to teams since 2022.

But let's go back to nutrition for a moment, focusing on the people who act as the link between nutritionist and rider. Once upon a time they handed out *musettes* at feed zones and in the evenings gave massages. On their paycheque they were called *soigneur*, but are now known as a 'sports assistant'. Like many others Alain Bizet, after a brief stint as a professional cyclist with Fangio (1983) and Coop (1984), gave up his cycling shorts to work directly behind a massage table. He started in 1985 with the great Renault team, and 40 years later he's still on the front line, most recently with the French track cycling team at the Paris Olympics. A crucial link in the food chain, he explains: 'It's our responsibility before the start of a stage to prepare two personalised water bottles for each rider. They contain between 40 and 80 grams of sugar and mineral salts, following an app. Instead of the good old-fashioned feed zone with its *musettes* containing *tartelette de riz* (rice pudding), chicken sandwiches, fruit jellies, bananas and so on, there are now "extra-feed-zones", with bottles containing the same portions of carbohydrates, proteins and mineral salts. Distribution takes place every 15km. The rider receives information about the location on their onboard computer, which is fixed to the handlebars. This rendezvous is crucial because – due to high average speeds and to avoid unnecessary chases – it is infinitely preferable for a rider not to drop back to their *directeur sportif* for supplies. Added up, all these single-use water bottles make up the colossal figure of 2400 bottles per team over the course of a Tour de France. And with 20 teams at the start of the Tour, that makes 48,000 bottles in total.'

The other big innovation was the appearance of gels – so-called 'fast sugars'. Bizet again: 'More and more riders now wear only a skinsuit with no pockets at the back, so they keep their gels in their shorts. The skinsuit is like a second skin with no wrinkles. Every team is now on the hunt for marginal wattage gains. In hot weather it is common to distribute ice socks to riders. These are placed on the neck to lower body temperature by one or two degrees, again, always to gain watts. A watt here and a watt there – computer scientists have quantified these aerodynamic benefits, from new textiles to alloys and so on, at 20 per cent.'

The British Sky team, which later became Ineos (under the same governance), was the biggest pioneer in this technological revolution. Riders on the Ineos team, owned by billionaire Sir Jim Ratcliffe, were the first to turn up at races with a sleeper bus, where each rider had their own mattress, pillow and sheets. They were also the first to have a food-truck that would impress even a Michelin-starred chef. They were the first to install eight personalised washing machines on the team bus, complete with a massage table at the back. This saved precious minutes of rest, which accumulated into hours by the end of a Tour. After the micronutrition provided during the stage, in the evening at dinner the nutritionist takes over. Generally, the menu alternates between rice, pasta, eggs, fish or white meat, fruit and yoghurt. It's a classic menu, but everything is meticulously weighed. Anglo-Saxons no longer eat red meat. Too many toxins. Briek Schotte, 'the Last of the Flemings', who finished second in the 1948 Tour de France (behind Bartali) and a great Classics hunter (winning the Tour of Flanders in 1942 and 1948), would have had something to say about that. In his farm near Kanegem, West Flanders, his father used to have a cow slaughtered at the start of the Spring Classics season. And so the young man would take the train the day before Paris–Roubaix, bringing his bike and a rucksack in which his father had stuffed a large steak from the cow. 'Hang on to this, he told the cook when he arrived at the hotel. Cook it for me tomorrow morning at 6 a.m.'

Slovenian Tadej Pogačar in the yellow jersey during the 2024 Tour de France

SUCCESSORS

During the writing of this book, I created a survey. I asked 100 current or former professional and amateur cyclists, as well as journalists from different countries, to rank the top 10 greatest cyclists in history, across all eras. The result was striking. Of the 96 responses, Eddy Merckx was the number one 91 times, and number two the other five. Bernard Hinault was first three times, Fausto Coppi twice. It's interesting to note that 'The Badger' (Hinault) was ranked second 46 times and third 47 times. '*Il Campionissimo*' (Coppi) was ranked second 45 times and third 49 times. Jacques Anquetil was most often ranked between fourth and seventh. He was ahead of Felice Gimondi, Tadej Pogačar, Miguel Induráin, Louison Bobet, Gino Bartali and Rik Van Looy. Next comes a 'grouped' peloton made up of: Chris Froome, Bernard Thévenet, Roger De Vlaeminck, Greg LeMond, Alberto Contador, Sean Kelly, Joop Zoetemelk, Mathieu van der Poel, Freddy Maertens, Rik Van Steenbergen, Jan Janssen, Stephen Roche, Luis Ocaña, Johan Museeuw, Lucien Van Impe, Raymond Poulidor, Alfredo Binda, Federico Bahamontes, Tony Rominger, Vincenzo Nibali, Alejandro Valverde, Marco Pantani and Antonin Magne.

Eddy Merckx's career wasn't just a list of victories; it was a redefinition of what was possible in professional cycling, and it left an indelible mark on the sport. His list of achievements is so extraordinary that it often feels like an anomaly, a historical aberration. Was it a source of inspiration for the generations that came after him? Five former champions – one Dutch, one French, one Belgian, one Italian and one Spanish, all Monument winners – gave their vision and perception of the 'phenomenon'.

However, the events of the 2024 Tour de France, which thrust Tadej Pogačar into the spotlight after his victory, have made him more than just an heir. At 26, the Slovenian is positioning himself as a potential successor to The Cannibal. To his quadruple in the Tour de France (2020, 2021, 2024, 2025) and a Giro d'Italia (2024), he has added 10 Monuments: Liège–Bastogne–Liège (2021, 2024, 2025), Tour of Lombardy (five wins, 2021–2025 inclusive) and the Tour of Flanders (2023, 2025). His aggressive style and hunger to race everything he can are admired by cycling legends such as Merckx, Hinault and Thévenet, who are seen as the traditional gatekeepers or standard-bearers of the sport. Pogačar has the pedigree, command and drive that are essential for a champion. He is clearly a rider poised to follow in the tracks of the sport's all-time greats.

Pogačar has the potential to equal or even surpass Merckx's five victories in the Tour de France. However, his chances of equalling Merckx's record in the Giro d'Italia are less certain as he would need to add four more wins. Equalling Merckx's multiple victories in the cobbled Classics such as Paris–Roubaix (where Pogačar has a 0/3 record) and Milan–San Remo (0/7) is improbable, unachievable even. And then, way up, is that pinnacle of 525 victories that neither Pogačar nor anyone else will ever reach. Because everything has changed; cycling has transformed from a sport with an average of 150 race days to around 50 per season.

Adrie van der Poel

Tour of Flanders 1986, Liège–Bastogne–Liège 1988

'The first time I heard the name Eddy Merckx was on the radio, and I must have been 9 or 10. We lived on a farm and worked most of the time. I really liked cycling and I took part in a few races, but I was truly awful. I was overtaken by everyone. The only reason I continued was because I liked it. But I grew up; I went from the juniors to the amateurs. One day, as fate would have it, I met Rini Wagtmans, a former teammate of Merckx and the Dutch national team selector. I still wasn't winning, but he said, 'You have something, you'll be able to ride in international races.' Wagtmans selected me for the 1979 Amateur World Championships in Valkenburg, where I crashed. After that I competed in the 1980 Moscow Olympics, finishing seventh – the first European. Then, in 1981, I turned professional. So where does Merckx fit into all this? He was a great rider. Incredible list of achievements. There were 14 years between us and I never rode with him. In 1978 when he retired I was just starting to make some headway as an amateur. I knew he had a huge record of victories. He was so impressive that when you were young it was almost unreal; there was no comparison.

'In 1981, the year of my first professional contract, he was no longer still racing, but you could feel his presence. Merckx was everywhere: in the Classics, on the Grand Tours. I'd heard about him too because I was on the same team as Joop Zoetemelk, who taught me the most as a person. He was one of the most intelligent riders on a bike: honest and respectful, and that really matters in life. I also share his philosophy of the sport. In 1986, my first victory of the season was the Tour of Flanders, which Merckx won twice. And in 1988 I won Liège–Bastogne–Liège, which Merckx won five times. But it never crossed my mind that I had to win three, four or five of them. I trained hard, I was serious and the main thing was that I did what I could do well. I only had one chance to wear the yellow jersey – at the start of the 1984 Tour de France – and I didn't let it slip through my fingers. I took it as a reward for my hard work. Personally, my only regret from that time is that I never got to truly enjoy my victories in peace. You had to race all the time. I was racing 140 days a year; today they do between 50 and 70. The sport has changed, the bikes have changed, the world has changed. And yes, of course, Eddy Merckx was the strongest and the best, but, I would clarify – for his era. That 1970s generation – Merckx, De Vlaeminck, Maertens and others – and even the 1980s generation – Hinault, Kuiper, Thévenet, Kelly, Moser and so on – all made cycling history. But today's generation, with riders like Pogačar, Mathieu (his son), van Aert and Vingegaard will also leave a lasting legacy that will be remembered for years to come. But I seriously think that Pogačar, who is still so young, may well be able to match Merckx's achievements.'

Marc Madiot

Paris–Roubaix 1985 and 1991

'Eddy Merckx is the rider I hated the most in the world when I was a kid. The first time I saw him he was scouting some stages of the 1970 Tour de France for RTL. It was in Renazé on a Sunday, a day of communion, just as people were leaving the church. He rode past the RTL car in his Faemino jersey. It was the first time I saw him in the flesh. It was like seeing a living legend – a god – go past. Truly majestic. After that I had the chance to see him again in criteriums, in Bain-de-Bretagne for example with Gimondi, who was so elegant and refined on a bike. With Merckx it was strength and raw power. My biggest regret is that I never had the chance to see Ocaña race in person. He was my idol. Back then when we played, it was: "I'll be Ocaña, you can be Merckx." I used to cut out strips of paper and draw the team logos on them with coloured pencils, based on the Panini album. We'd pin them on our shirts. Mine was orange, like the Bic jersey. Molteni was a friend, Patrick Gaultier. He later became the mayor of Renazé. My brother Yvon was Poulidor.

'Much, much later, I told Merckx about it. It must have been at a riders' reunion, could have been Régnié-Durette in Beaujolais. I finally spoke freely late at night, and Jean-Pierre Danguillaume was an eye-witness. I actually came out with: "You know, Eddy, you are the guy I detested most in the world. I was a huge fan of Ocaña." And I added: "But now that I know you, I admire you." And when I see him these days, I greet him as the living god of our sport.

I talk to him informally ("tu" not "vous"), because I think I've earned that right, being in the same profession. But deep down I still hold that mark of respect, as if I were meeting the president. Eddy – he's a good guy in every respect. One day when I was looking for a cycling clothing partner for my team and – by coincidence – I was on the phone with him. Without knowing what I was up to, he said to me, "If you need a supplier for your riders, I know one who could do the job. You can tell him I suggested you call." Twenty years on, and I'm still with Alé.

'Merckx gave me some of my most intense feelings and memories as a kid. For me the Menté stage was a truly dramatic event. On that Orcières stage my heart was beating like a madman. Until recently the only sounds I had in my head were voices from the radio. Radio is magical; it lets your imagination run wild. I had the chance to do a bit on a radio show and it's absolutely brilliant. You can put an image in people's minds. And Orcières 1971 – I still have those voices in my head. What Luis did that day was the greatest moment in the history of cycling. It will never be bettered. Everyone thought the Tour was done and dusted, but the next day Eddy was back in the fight. And then came the day after that: at home it was harvest-time and we always stopped everything for the stage finish. The day of Menté was one of utter despair, complete devastation – heartbreak for a child. Afterwards, I have to admit I had an incredible stroke of luck. I got to take part in the same sport as the greats, to meet them and to hear them talk about their lives. The first time I won Paris–Roubaix I was going through the village of Hem, not far from Roubaix. At that moment two thoughts crossed my mind. One was for my friend Alain Bondue, who lives in Hem, and I said to myself, "Damn! I bet Alain would give anything to be in my place right now." And a little further on, when I was sure I was going to win, I said to myself, "Man, right now you're doing what Merckx and De Vlaeminck did." That sent shivers down my spine – and then it was over.

'You can say what you like, but for me the Merckx generation was the golden age, a truly legendary era of cycling.'

Fons De Wolf

Tour of Lombardy 1980, Milan–San Remo 1981

'Merckx and I only crossed paths, without truly seeing each other. His career ended in 1978 and I went professional in 1979. I'm going to be perfectly honest: I admired him, but his career was not a source of inspiration for me. At 13, a kid dreams of being like an idol who wins and loses. A child should be happy when their hero triumphs, but they also need to learn what it means to feel sadness when they lose. It is character-building. My idol was Roger De Vlaeminck, for his style and qualities as a Classics rider. Merckx was in a world of his own: unreal, inhuman, quite simply a god. He decided he was going to win, and he won – everywhere: Tour de France, Giro, rainbow jersey, Monuments. Who wants to be like – or takes themselves – for a god?

'You need to have your dreams almost within reach. There should be an element of the impossible in dreams, but you have to be able to have some belief, too. I thought I was on the right track to becoming a good rider. I won

the Tour of Flanders juniors in 1974, the Paris–Roubaix
and the Belgian Amateur Championship in 1978. When I
turned pro in 1979, I had a bright future ahead after victories in Lombardy in 1980 and Milan–San Remo in 1981,
second place at Liège–Bastogne–Liège in 1982, two Het
Volkes in 1982 and 1983 and a Tour de France stage win
in 1984. But never, not even in my greatest moments, did
I feel like Eddy's shadow was looming over me. I didn't
even think about him for a moment when I triumphed
in the Milan–San Remo, a race he won seven times. Two
Monuments felt good; it was a reward – a statement – but I
had that clarity, and I knew my limits. But the Grand Tours
weren't for me, even with a decent early record. I never
had a problem riding as a *domestique* when needed – no
questions asked.

'In 1980, I found myself at the Boule D'Or team alongside Roger DeVlaeminck. I gave a lot for him. My mentality
must have suited him because he promised to return the
favour someday. That chance came when he took over as
directeur sportif at Tonton Tapis, but he had forgotten everything and insisted that there had never been any question
of an agreement between us. There's the rider and there
is the man. For me, your word is your word and a gentleman should never break it. But Merckx wasn't like that.
I never rode alongside him in the peloton but after my
career ended I had the immense pleasure of being a part of
his group and riding with him and his teammates during
the week. At the end of that was the best beer I ever tasted.
I even rode in Merckx's cycling shorts one day when I'd
forgotten my own. That's how I discovered the greatest
rider – in every sense of the word – of all time.

'Dreaming of being Merckx is like dreaming of winning the lottery. Maybe one day Tadej Pogačar – an aggressive rider I like – will do as well as him in the Tour de France, the Giro or Liège. Four Tours de France by the age of 26 is very good. But he will never reach Eddy's record. There will never be another Merckx. These days riders spend too much time training, preparing. On the other hand, their monitoring has become highly professional. At the finish of a Tour stage, there are eight *soigneurs* – one for each rider – and they immediately give them a personalised recovery drink. If I made just one comparison with the current generation, I'd say that to make a Merckx you'd need to combine the qualities of Pogačar and van der Poel. But what was truly unique about Merckx – what struck me the most – was his mentality. He would rather die than lose. And that's where I'm really looking to see what Pogačar is made of.'

Gianni Bugno

Milan–San Remo 1990, Tour of Flanders 1994

'Before I started cycling I played football and did a bit of swimming. Then, at 15, because I had friends who were racing, I decided to give it a try. My first race was in the rain. I got caught with a kilometre to go, but I was sure I'd have another go – and I didn't stop until 1998. I had a professional career that lasted 14 years. The first time I heard the name Eddy Merckx was around the time I'd just got my license, but he was no longer racing. People spoke of him like some kind of alien. Some said he was better than Coppi, but not everyone agreed. It's always like that. Every generation has its own great champion. Mine was Hinault because he seemed real. I saw him on television. I followed his interviews closely. Hinault won his first Tour de France when I started cycling. Merckx was already part of history. I never saw him race, and your idol can't be someone who only exists in stories told by old-timers. I admired Hinault for his way of riding, his direct character – simply because he was Hinault. I have a precise memory, which may seem a bit ordinary but will stay with me forever. I took part in my first Paris–Brussels in 1986 and I knew it was Hinault's last race. It was the first time I saw him in the flesh and I went to shake his hand. Just to tell him, *complimenti* (congratulations).

'To begin with I did a lot of track cycling. I won pursuits, Madisons and eliminations. It was an excellent training ground. I was the Italian champion in individual pursuit as a junior and an amateur, and I must say that when I turned professional everything I learned on the track – positioning, quick reflexes – served me well. But I never once thought about attacking the hour record. Induráin was in a league of his own and that quickly brought me back down to earth. As my career progressed I realised that what Merckx had done in the Giro, the Tour, Milan–San Remo and elsewhere made him a champion in a class of his own. Next to him, even if you won a Tour of Flanders, a Giro or a Milan–San Remo, you felt small, crushed by his achievements. When you look at it like that, he is the greatest. Merckx is Pelé or Maradona. He made history in sport, not just cycling. Judging by his achievements, he's undeniably the greatest of all and I believe he always will be.

'But you can't compare him to Coppi. Because Coppi is a legend and a legend can't be compared to anyone. In mythology, you don't compare one god with another. They are gods and that's it. I agree with the old-timers when they say Coppi was like radio, Merckx was like television. With radio, you listen and you imagine. Listening to a Coppi race on the radio is very different than seeing a Merckx race on RAI. There's no point trying; you'll never settle the debate between those who prefer Coppi to Merckx, or the other way round.'

Óscar Freire

Milan–San Remo 2004, 2007, 2010

'I can't remember the first time I met Merckx. Probably after a race I won in Belgium, perhaps the Brabantse Pijl. There were so many other times: a Milan–San Remo, a team presentation, a UCI gathering of former world champions. There are 31 years between us. I was born in 1976, the year of his last victory in a Milan–San Remo. Three generations separate us – an entire world. I rode with a Merckx – but it was Eddy's son.

'It will come as no surprise to anyone when I say that cycling isn't the same sport any more, and my three victories in Milan–San Remo can't really compare to his seven wins. You must have truly extraordinary qualities to win *La Primavera* seven times. Merckx was amazing. He made a difference everywhere: on the flats, in the mountains, in the Tours, in the Classics – even on the track. When I see his list of achievements I am simply speechless. No one will ever equal it. But back then the roads and the gear were suited to that style of racing. It was more of a feat to say, "I beat Merckx" than "I won the race".'

'The "three wise men" are our Father Christmas in Spain, and they gave me my first bike in 1985 when I was nine years old. It was garnet-red with iron tubing. In that same year my first club was the Galon Cycling Club of Torrelavega. Their jersey was yellow. Before me, no one in my family had ever raced or even been interested in sport, and I'd never heard of Bernard Hinault, who I believe won his fifth Tour de France in 1985. So, as you can imagine I knew absolutely nothing about Merckx, and that didn't change for a long time. Much later, when I became world champion for the first of my three titles in 1999, it also never crossed my mind – unlike with my three Milan–San Remos – to say to myself, "You've emulated Merckx." My way of riding was very different from his. My repertoire was also quite limited: I was always in the sprint and in a small group. He was excellent everywhere: mountains, sprint, solo. I would never dare say that I was an heir to Merckx or Hinault.

'I was at the cusp of two eras: the time of Kelly and Hinault, and the current one with Alaphilippe and Pogačar. But Merckx's time is just too far away for me to relate to. In 1999 equipment was evolving rapidly, but there were still a few surprises. In Lisbon at the 1999 World Championships, an hour before the start I couldn't stand my cycling shoes any more. They were squashing my feet. The pain was excruciating and I didn't have a spare pair. So I simply cut them open with a knife to free my big toe. Today, something like that would never happen. Riders essentially slide their feet into slippers and their bikes are also lighter, more aero-dynamic and much faster. New training methods and all the technology have levelled the playing field. It's become increasingly difficult to surprise an opponent and break away. That's why I'm proud to be the only rider of the last two decades to win the Milan–San Remo multiple times. Conversely in Merckx's era, physical qualities had such a direct impact on performance. Merckx was like a car from Formula 1; the others were Formula 2 or Formula 3.'

Merckx during the 1970 Tour de France between Gap and Mont Ventoux

OUT ON HIS OWN

'May he live a thousand years!'

CHINESE PROVERB

Surely, within Eddy Merckx's immense, Babylonian list of victories – 525 wins, Grand Tours, Monuments, Classics – there was a flaw. It was the Paris–Tours. He took part in it six times and his best result was sixth. Only Rik Van Looy managed the Grand Slam and won everything. That hasn't prevented Merckx from being long enshrined in legend, even attaining mythical status during his lifetime. He has become the ultimate benchmark, a unit of comparison, a champion who transcended generations and even withstood the revolution that has transformed cycling. He dominated the sport for years in the 1970s on all terrains and in all weathers, to such an extent that people started referring to that era as Merckxism, the way in modern art they refer to Cubism. Bringing together the testimonials that form the common thread of this investigation, we've come to the conclusion that the deep-seated driving force behind Merckxism was his endless pursuit of victory. For him, a rest was time wasted; moving on to new horizons was living the life he'd dreamed of. Merckx was constantly moving. He circumnavigated the planet 12 times! Does that power, tactical sense and intelligence mean he is the Greatest Of All Time? Judging by his achievements – and in the eyes of everyone we have heard from – he is, without a doubt. Merckx is to cycling what Pelé is to football, Ayrton Senna to F1 or Muhammad Ali to boxing. The question of the 'GOAT' has been raised for all of these legends, but the answers are more nuanced, sparking passionate discussions because comparisons between generations is so difficult.

Some believe, for example, that without his 18 months of military service during the Second World War, deprived of training and competition, Fausto Coppi would be without equal. And then there are those who worship Merckx as a legendary, almost otherworldly, champion in a league of his own. Everyone thinks they are right. This debate is pointless, but it does have one significant benefit: it lets us bring back memories of our childhood, youth and the Tour de France. We all know that the champions of our childhood stay with us our whole lives.

Eddy Merckx is such a memory for tens of thousands of children who grew up with his exploits, who played at being Merckx on their bikes, who – because of him – pinned on a race number. Even today, Merckx is the figure of dreams that is evoked whenever a Belgian rider wins a Classic.

What we can also say without fear of contradiction is that the Tour de France was the foundation of his career. You must remember that the tidal wave from Brussels celebrated his first yellow jersey in Paris in 1969. For millions of people, those images of July – waiting by the road to see the Tour de France pass – are their eternal memories of youth. We won't go into a nostalgic lament about the enormous changes that have revolutionised cycling. Today's young successors to Merckx have – from childhood – been part of the Nintendo, PlayStation or Pokémon generation. They are digital natives who have grown up with social media, marketing techniques and image rights. Their daily professional lives are filled with PowerPoints, data, power meters, altitude training, watts and so on. Twenty-first-century cycling won't be going back. Merckx would still hold a significant, though less visible, place in it, since he'd only be able to race an average of 50 days a year.

That's not the Merckx we want. The Merckx we love stormed through life, relentlessly pushing forward and leaving an incredible trail of victories in his wake. He is honoured in the *Guinness Book of Records* as well as *Sports Illustrated*. 'The Majesty of Monsieur Merckx' was the headline of the famous American magazine, saying, 'Belgium's incomparable Eddy is sovereign of his sport ... [he] has made Merckxists of the masses throughout the world ... there are two Eddy Merckxes: One is the cold, deadpan killer cyclist. The other ... is congenial, outgoing and something of a chatterbox.' Backed by polls, Eddy is considered to be one of the greatest Belgians of all time in his home country. He is second only to Father Damien, a heroic missionary who dedicated his life to caring for lepers on the island of Molokai, Tahiti.

Two reflections capture perfectly the champion and the passion he ignited. Jacques Goddet, in his capacity as director of the Tour de France, votes for Coppi: 'Number one in terms of results is Eddy Merckx. But for me someone stands above him, and that is Fausto Coppi, who performed under circumstances that seemed superhuman – almost divine – given his physique and natural ability.'

Louis Caput, a former French road champion who later became the *directeur sportif* for Raymond Poulidor, Joop Zoetemelk and Cyrille Guimard, argues in favour of Merckx: 'I consider Rik Van Looy to be the greatest Classics rider among those I had the opportunity to judge. Furthermore, I consider Fausto Coppi to be the number one stage racer. Eddy Merckx was Van Looy plus Coppi.'

Finally, how can we resist bringing up this reflection from Luis Ocaña for future generations? In the late 1980s, in an interview with *L'Équipe* magazine, the ephemeral yellow jersey wearer of the 1971 Tour – born in the same year and month, just a week apart from the rider who vanquished him – recalled this:

'I'd like young people to truly understand who Eddy was. We weren't able to just casually stop for a pee like I see [cyclists] do now. I often had to go in my bike shorts.'

Perhaps one day, Eddy's inscription will read, as a tribute: 'He was not just a champion, he was an entire world.' On 15 June, 2025, Eddy Merckx celebrated his 80th birthday. 'May he live a thousand years!' as the Chinese proverb says.

Merckx (L) and his son Axel (R), who turned professional under
the Motorola jersey, participate in a charity race in Liège in 1993

*Merckx, who crossed the summit of the Tourmalet first ahead of his teammate
Martin Van Den Bossche, would go on to seal the 1969 Tour's fate with
a victorious 140km solo breakaway during the 17th Luchon–Mourenx stage*

AFTERWORD BY EDDY MERCKX

You ask me if I could see myself cycling today? It's not easy to say yes. Everything is so different, it has all changed so much. Everything is calculated, digitised, directed. I won my first World Championship title on a completely standard bike, it wasn't customised at all. I'm not against progress – quite the opposite, I'm in favour of modernisation. But what shocks me about this new cycling is that riders spend months without racing. I would have struggled to go along with that. Where is the pleasure for the rider if not competing in races? Mathieu van der Poel started the 2024 Tour de France with nine days of racing in his legs. That would have been positively unthinkable in my day. I had to race all the time, everywhere – three times a day when I could. I competed in 150 race days a year on average; one year it was 195. When you're a rider, the pleasure comes from competing in all of them. I pursued a profession that was my passion. It wasn't just a job, and I did it out of love for cycling.

Passion has guided my entire career, my whole life. I relied on the moral values that my parents instilled in me: respect, humility and hard work. They stayed with me my entire career and afterwards. Education plays a big part in shaping who we are, and I never claimed to be the best. My parents instilled in me a fundamental rule: always look up, not down. To become a champion, humility is essential. But what's passed down also includes the genes. I won't deny it – genetically I received something from my parents, my grandparents, maybe even further back, that others don't have.

If I had to do it all over again how would I race, and what mistake would I not repeat? My way of riding would be the same. When you let yourself be guided you're no longer yourself. I won five Tours de France – it's something I'm immensely proud of. Time has passed and it is 50 years since my last victory in 1974. I fought hard and I gave everything to win a sixth, but I look back without yearning: I have no regrets. Maybe I should have ridden the 1973 Tour, but that's just a footnote – and besides, those who aren't there are always in the wrong. Well – that's that. I'm the happiest man alive with my five Tours de France, five Giros, a Vuelta, all the Classics, my World Championship titles and an hour record. What is wonderful is that 50 years on, rivalries have become friendships. My fiercest rivals became my friends and my teammates have remained just that. That's one of the great lessons life teaches us afterwards. There's a lot of warmth in the reunions with old riders, and what happened 50 years ago no longer matters. If there's one mistake I wouldn't repeat it was continuing the Tour de France in 1975 after I had a crash at the start in Valloire. A double fracture of the jaw is serious and then there's the trauma on top of it. I didn't know if it was day or night, someone told me I was speaking Flemish to a Spanish rider. I should have dropped out instead of clinging on. I was crazy to keep going. I was never the same again after that Tour.

You ask who my toughest opponent was, and today, who comes closest to sharing my mindset? I lined up at the start of every race, on every kind of terrain. Roger De Vlaeminck and Walter Godefroot were major contenders in the Classics, but the one who was there everywhere – all the time on every kind of terrain – was Felice Gimondi.

Today, Tadej Pogačar is the one who stands out. He rides, he wins, he loses, he starts again. He races everything he possibly can – and he's absolutely right. That's how I see cycling.

How would I like to be remembered when I'm gone? Above all, I'd like to be seen as an example for young people. To tell them that the most important thing is to stay true to themselves, to keep their feet on the ground and to enjoy themselves even when they're struggling. Cycling is a life lesson. Whether my name fades or is forgotten, that's just how time works. For people to remember me would be a form of recognition. But it's not for us to decide.

L to R: Merckx, Felice Gimondi and Vittorio Adorni during the Giro d'Italia in 1969

MERCKX'S ACHIEVEMENTS

Merckx's Victories Year by Year

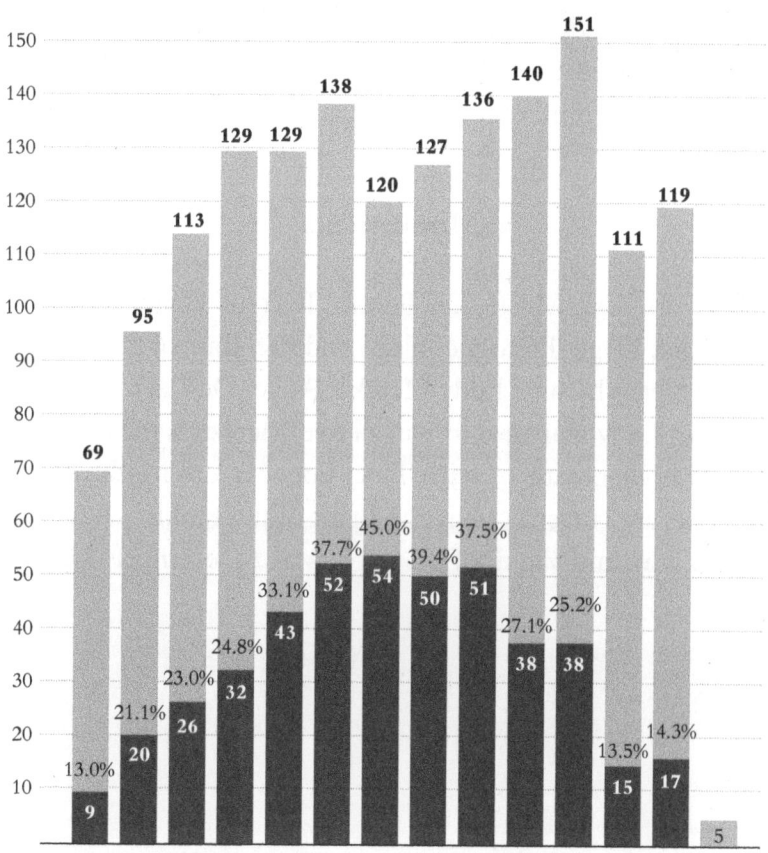

Dark grey = number of wins. Light grey = number of race days.

The percentage indicates wins compared to the number of races.

1971 was his most successful season: 54 wins from 120 days of racing.

Merckx calculated that he was travelling 35,000km per season with the exception of the first (1965) and last (1978). Including the other 12 seasons (1966 to 1977), that makes 420,000km. Adding the junior and amateur years means Merckx passed the milestone of 500,000km. That is 12.5 times the circumference of the Earth.

Monuments

There are five: Milan–San Remo, Tour of Flanders, Paris–Roubaix, Liège–Bastogne–Liège and the Tour of Lombardy. In the hierarchy, only Eddy Merckx, Roger De Vlaeminck and Rik Van Looy managed to win all five. Merckx is the absolute record holder, with 19 wins. Tadej Pogačar and Mathieu van der Poel are currently active and part of this ranking. Pogačar has 10 wins and van der Poel has 8 as of 2 December, 2025.

	Total	Milan–San Remo	Tour of Flanders	Paris–Roubaix	Liège–Bastogne–Liège	Tour of Lombardy
Eddy Merckx (BEL), 1966–1976	19	7	2	3	5	2
Roger De Vlaeminck (BEL), 1970–1979	11	3	1	4	1	2
Tadej Pogačar (SLO), since 2021	11	1	2	0	3	5
Sean Kelly (IRL), 1983–1992	9	2	0	2	2	3
Fausto Coppi (ITA), 1946–1954	9	3	0	1	0	5
Rik Van Looy (BEL), 1958–1965	8	1	2	3	1	1
Mathieu van der Poel (NLD), since 2020	8	2	3	3	0	0
Fabian Cancellara (SWI), 2006–2014	7	1	3	3	0	0
Tom Boonen (BEL), 2004–2012	7	0	3	4	0	0
Gino Bartali (ITA), 1936–1950	7	4	0	0	0	3
Bernard Hinault (FRA), 1977–1984	5	0	0	1	2	2
Philippe Gilbert (BEL), 2009–2019	5	0	1	1	1	2

Rankings accurate as of 31/03/2026. Between the two wars – 1918 to 1928 – Costante Girardengo (ITA) won 6 Milan–San Remo and 3 Giro di Lombardia in his Italian homeland.

Grand Tour Winners

Seven riders have won the Giro, the Tour de France and the Vuelta – the three Grand Tours on the calendar. In chronological order, they are: Jacques Anquetil, Felice Gimondi, Eddy Merckx, Bernard Hinault, Alberto Contador, Vincenzo Nibali and Christopher Froome.

Only four have won five Tours de France: Anquetil, Merckx, Hinault and Induráin; three have won five Giros: Binda, Coppi and Merckx. The first American to add his name on the list of the Tour de France winners was Greg LeMond (1986). The first South American to triumph at the Tour is the Colombian Egan Bernal (2019). The Australian Cadel Evans was the first racer from Oceania to win the Tour de France (2011).

Total	Cyclist	Tour de France	Giro d'Italia	Vuelta a España
11	Eddy Merckx (1968–1974)	5	5	1
10	Bernard Hinault (1978–1985)	5	3	2
8	Jacques Anquetil (1957–1964)	5	2	1
7	Fausto Coppi (1940–1953)	2	5	0
7	Miguel Induráin (1992–2005)	5	2	0
7	Alberto Contador (2007–2015)	2	3	2
7	Chris Froome (2011–2018)	4	1	2
5	Gino Bartali (1936–1948)	2	3	0
5	Felice Gimondi (1965–1976)	1	3	1
5	Tadej Pogačar (2020–)	4	1	0
4	Tony Rominger (1992–1995)	0	1	3
4	Roberto Heras (2000–2005)	0	0	4
4	Vincenzo Nibali (2010–2018)	1	2	1
4	Primož Roglič (2019–)	0	1	3
3	Louison Bobet (1953–1955)	3	0	0
3	Charly Gaul (1956–1959)	1	2	0
3	Laurent Fignon (1983–1989)	2	1	0
3	Pedro Delgado (1985–1989)	1	0	2
3	Greg LeMond (1986–1990)	3	0	0

Days in the yellow jersey (from the Second World War to the end of the 2024 Tour)

I	Eddy Merckx (BEL)	97
2	Bernard Hinault (FRA)	76
3	Miguel Induráin (SPA)	60
4	Chris Froome (GBR)	59
5	Tadej Pogačar (SLO)	54
6	Jacques Anquetil (FRA)	51
7	Louison Bobet (FRA)	34
8	Fabian Cancellara (SWI)	29
9	Jonas Vingegaard (DEN)	27
10	René Vietto (FRA)	26
II	Laurent Fignon (FRA)	22
II	Joop Zoetemelk (NDR)	22
13	Greg LeMond (USA)	21.5
14	Gino Bartali (ITA)	20
14	Thomas Voeckler (FRA)	20
16	Fausto Coppi (ITA)	19
16	Vincenzo Nibali (ITA)	19
18	Felice Gimondi (ITA)	18
18	Jan Ullrich (GER)	18
20	Rudi Altig (GER)	17.5
21	Luis Ocaña (SPA)	17
21	Roger Pingeon (FRA)	17
23	André Darrigade (FRA)	16.5
24	Bernard Thévenet (FRA)	16
25	Dietrich Thurau (GER)	15.5
26	Geraint Thomas (GBR)	15
27	Julian Alaphilippe (FRA)	14
27	Pedro Delgado (SPA)	14
27	Bradley Wiggins (GBR)	14
27	Gastone Nencini (ITA)	14
27	Bjarne Riis (DEN)	14
32	Andy Schleck (LUX)	13

Wearers from before the war: Antonin Magne (FRA), 38 days; Nicolas Frantz (LUX), 37; André Leducq (FRA), 34.5; Ottavio Bottecchia (ITA), 34; Sylvère Maes (BEL), 26.

Stage wins on the Tour

Mark Cavendish (GBR)	35
Eddy Merckx (BEL)	34
Bernard Hinault (FRA)	28
André Darrigade (FRA)	22
Tadej Pogačar (SLO)	17
Jacques Anquetil (FRA)	16
Freddy Maertens (BEL)	15
Marcel Kittel (GER)	14
Gino Bartali (ITA)	12
Mario Cippollini (ITA)	
Miguel Induráin (SPA)	
Robbie McEwen (AU)	
Peter Sagan (SLO)	
Erik Zabel (GER)	
Louison Bobet (FRA)	11
André Greipel (GER)	
Charly Gaul (LUX)	10
Walter Godefroot (BEL)	
Gerrie Knetemann (NDR)	
Jan Raas (NDR)	
Joop Zoetemelk (NDR)	
Thor Hushovd (NOR)	

Pre-war notable winners:

André Leducq (FRA)	25
Nicolas Frantz (LUX)	20
François Faber (LUX)	19
Jean Alavoine (FRA)	17
René Le Grevès (FRA)	16
Charles Pélissier (FRA)	
Philippe Thys (BEL)	13
Louis Trousselier (FRA)	12
Jean Aerts (BEL)	11
Raffael Di Paco (ITA)	
Antonin Magne (FRA)	10
Henri Pélissier (FRA	

Record for wins in the mountains

Tadej Pogačar	14
Eddy Merckx	10
Gino Bartali	9
Marco Pantani	8
Charly Gaul	7
Federico Bahamontes	
Lucien Van Impe	
Fausto Coppi	6
Luis Ocaña	
Joop Zoetemelk	

Record for time trial wins

Bernard Hinault	20
Eddy Merckx	16
Jacques Anquetil	11

Record for stage victories in a single Tour

Eddy Merckx	8 (1970 and 1974)
Freddy Maertens	8 (1976 and 1978)

Largest gap at the finish of the Tour de France

Difference	Year	Cyclists
28'17"	1952	1. Fausto Coppi (ITA) 2. Stan Ockers (BEL)
26'16"	1948	1. Gino Bartali (ITA) 2. Briek Schotte (BEL)
22'00"	1951	1. Hugo Koblet (SWI) 2. Raphaël Géminiani (FRA)
17'54"	1969	1. Eddy Merckx (BEL) 2. Roger Pingeon (FRA)
15'51"	1973	1. Luis Ocaña (SPA) 2. Bernard Thévenet (FRA)
15'49"	1954	1. Louison Bobet (FRA) 2. Ferdi Kübler (SWI)
14'56"	1957	1. Jacques Anquetil (FRA) 2. Marcel Janssens (BEL)
14'34"	1981	1. Bernard Hinault (FRA) 2. Lucien Van Impe (BEL)
14'18"	1953	1. Louison Bobet (FRA) 2. Jean Malléjac (FRA)
12'41"	1970	1. Eddy Merckx (BEL) 2. Joop Zoetemelk (NDR)
12'14"	1961	1. Jacques Anquetil (FRA) 2. Guido Carlesi (ITA)
10'55"	1949	1. Fausto Coppi (ITA) 2. Gino Bartali (ITA)
10'41"	1972	1. Eddy Merckx (BEL) 2. Felice Gimondi (ITA)
10'32"	1984	1. Laurent Fignon (FRA) 2. Bernard Hinault (FRA)

*Merckx speaking to journalists after winning
the Paris–Roubaix race with a 5-minute lead*

MERCKX MUSINGS

The Three Commandments by Andy McGrath

When I got into cycling as a teenager in the early 2000s, there were three commandments passed down to me: shave your legs, do not overlap the wheel in front and remember that Eddy Merckx is the greatest cyclist who ever lived.

While I am not even close to recalling his awe-inspiring athletic feats, there are far more people on the planet now who were not around for them either. So, you see, most of those born after his career's end don't have a choice. A bit like learning to wait for the green man at traffic lights or tying shoelaces, we are automatically Merckxists. (Roger De Vlaeminck must be fuming.)

Therefore, he has occupied a peculiar, dual place in my consciousness. It is difficult to square the gracefully ageing, ambassadorial man with the superheroic myth, the cut-glass cheekbones and majestic attacks helping to romanticise humdrum places like Mourenx and Meerbeke.

I have been fortunate enough to interview Merckx several times, dined with him, observed him for a day at his eponymous sportive in Austria. He has mischievously sung me the first bars of the Rolling Stones' 'Satisfaction' (even if that feeling was an enemy of voracity) with surprising tunefulness, and took all the time in the world to talk to young fans, much more teddy Merckx than 'The Cannibal'.

But I do not doubt that the beast still lurks. One day, he was saying Tadej Pogačar was better and anointing him as the greatest, the next recanting his opinion. After all these years, what Merckx says still matters to us journalists.

We might look for comparisons but pitting Merckx against anyone, let alone 1969 against 2020, is a fool's errand – woollen jerseys, summers of 40 criteriums, stars racing Six Days, the moon landing and The Beatles at number one: all gone and never coming back.

However, Merckx is somehow able to bridge time. Spaces he occupies in the here and now normally carry an electric charge. People walk around thinking, *is it really him?* Champion modern cyclists are shorn of ego and like shy children in his presence, as if meeting Father Christmas. He is like every cyclist's grandfather: we automatically crave respect and crave his approval.

His achievements and aura, this masterful book, the entire canon of collective cycling storytelling, all help to make Merckx immortal, but he is only flesh and blood. 'If I die, well, everyone dies. I'm not afraid of death,' he told me, months before his 70th birthday in 2015.

When he finally draws his last breath, I will make a pilgrimage to Brussels and try in vain to hop generations like he does. In my mind's eye, I have a photograph from the 1969 Tour de France to mirror: Merckx looking out from a balcony on the Grand-Place thronged with well-wishers chanting his name. In the Belgian capital, I will take in the scene with his friends, countrypeople, bike racers past and present, luminaries, all commingled in mourning him and what he represented – a thousand different meanings to a thousand different people. It will be like St Peter's Square after the death of the Pope, only there can be no successor this time.

Andy McGrath is the author of *Tadej Pogačar: Unstoppable.*

Number 1 by Carlton Kirby

There is a bar on the corner of the central square in Oudenaarde. It's hard to gain entry on Flanders day because it is brimful of cycling's heroes, with the rest of the world held back by security. Inside is a club meet of sorts; informal, you might say. Entry requirements? Be a god. The atmosphere is always relaxed. It's catch-up time for cycling deity.

Sean Kelly talking about Fabian Cancellara in 2014: 'Have you seen his numbers?'

Eddy Merckx: 'There is only one number that counts... 1...'

And right there you have it.

Eddy Merckx had only one way of being. And that was to be the best. Nothing else mattered. And to be the best there could be no compromise. Often unorthodox and always independent-minded, he was a maverick. Yet he wasn't a rule breaker, he was a rule maker ... of which there was only one strict rule. One he applied only to himself. 'Ride. A lot.' And he did.

Nobody trained harder, rode harder, and ultimately won harder than Eddy Merckx. Even winning wasn't enough it seemed. After all he was winning everything; on road, track, cycle-cross. Grand Tours, Monuments, Classics and stage races. Climbing, sprinting, time-trialling. Everything and in every way.

So in such a dominant position what become your targets? He began setting himself other goals and was livid if they slipped from his grasp. Beating himself was now the aim. He went for race records and personal bests. And if beating himself up was part of that, then so be it. Beating everyone else was simply a bi-product of his greatness.

Even for those off the bike he was hard to catch. Interviews were not common as he was so busy. Three-hundred-kilometre training rides for six or seven hours were quite the norm and began very early each morning. His disdain for rest days was famous. Eddy raced in full-blown competition for over 150 days per season ... the rest he spent training. How very un-modern.

Many ask how Eddy would fare in today's cycling world of planned season breaks, monitored nutrition and controlled training methods. Would he still be the best? The fact is, you have to take the margin of Eddy Merckx's achievements against the baseline of the greats he raced against. So far ahead of many amazing names was he that nothing has been seen like it since or possibly ever will be. And he did this not simply by using his considerable physical gifts, but by sheer bloody-minded determination to live by his own rule: Ride ... a lot.

So quite rightly we put Eddy Merckx on the tallest pedestal within cycling. The UCI mandates that the top step of a race podium should be at a height of 540mm... If we stack together all of Eddy's 525 professional career wins then you will find the great man standing at a height of just over 283.5m. That's quite the climb if you want to worship at his feet.

Carlton Kirby is the author of *Magic Spanner* and *Sticky Bottle*.

Milan–San Remo: The Arrival by Nige Tassell

Eddy Merckx wins the sprint ahead of Van Springel (R) and Durante (masked) and wins the first of his seven Milan–San Remo in 1966 © L'Équipe

It's just one of countless classic photographs of the greatest cyclist the world has ever known. But it was pretty much the first.

Many shots show him driving the peloton to break-ing point. Others might highlight a duel with a rival on a narrow mountain pass or yet another victory in a full-throttle sprint for the line. This particular photograph is one of the latter. Taken on Sunday 19 March, 1966, in a seaside town on the Italian Riviera, it shows the final second of that year's Milan–San Remo, the longest one-day race in professional cycling. More significantly, it shows the first of 19 Monument wins for this young man from the Brussels suburbs, a collection that, today, remains comfortably larger than that of anyone else.

That young man was Eddy Merckx.

The photograph, taken by a snapper risking life and limb by standing on Via Roma in Sanremo, just a few yards beyond the finish line, captures four riders charging for glory. Two are on the right-hand side of the road – 20-year-old Merckx and his compatriot Herman Vanspringel – and two are on the left – the Italians Adriano Durante and Michele Dancelli. Merckx's front wheel is both inches from the line and inches ahead of Durante's bike.

The younger Belgian, his elbows unconventionally splayed outwards at sharp angles as he thrusts his bike towards the white line, has joy etched all over his face. His mouth is breaking into a toothy grin, while his eyes widen in delight. Merckx's box-fresh Peugeot jersey – this was his debut season with the team – shines bright and white in the Italian sun. Across the street, Durante, pipped by the thinnest of margins, lets out a howl of despair.

But this win, captured so brilliantly by the fear-less photographer, was more than an announcement of Merckx's sprinting power in the final few hundred metres of a race. The previous six hours had shown that he wasn't simply the new speedball on the block, a man of electric pace on a home straight. It was further proof that he could also mix it on varied terrain and over gradients, having demonstrated just this throughout the eight-stage Paris–Nice the previous week. He had finished fourth in Nice, having enjoyed a spell in the leader's white jersey a few days earlier.

That afternoon in north-west Italy, Merckx had tracked the break of Raymond Poulidor over the coastal climb of Capo Berta before, on the final ascent of the day – the famous Poggio, just 5km from home – tossing down a gauntlet to the rest of the pack. With his head bobbing from side to side, he put the hammer down and pulled an increasingly fractured peloton up the hill. And he successfully broke them; only 10 other riders could stay with the pace he was setting towards the streets of Sanremo. And yet he still had enough in those thighs of his to see off Durante, Vanspringel and Dancelli on the final shakedown.

After this day, the world would start to know his name. In time, it would become a byword for sporting domination. Six letters, one syllable.

Merckx.

Back in March 1966, of course, the result wasn't an all-out declaration of the sport's new world order, nor a wholesale takeover of the peloton. It was merely a whisper of the young man's promise, a suggestion of the glory to come. Indeed, Merckx even seemed to have surprised himself by taking victory on Via Roma in what, at that point, was the longest race he'd ridden. He'd been in the saddle for more than 400 minutes.

'I had no idea how well I could do,' Merckx gushed in the post-race scrum, before declaring it to be his most pleasurable win to date, even eclipsing the world amateur title won in the French Alps two years earlier. 'I'm as happy today as when I pulled on the rainbow jersey in Sallanches. No, actually, I'm even happier.'

Back home in that Brussels suburb, someone else – watching the race on a flickering black-and-white TV screen rather than in the flesh on the Italian Riviera – was more than surprised. So the story goes, on seeing her eldest son first to the line, Merckx's mother Jenny promptly passed out. If that were her reaction every time Eddy won, the smelling salts would be in near-constant use over the following decade.

Nige Tassell is the author of *Three Weeks, Eight Seconds: Greg LeMond, Laurent Fignon and the Epic Tour de France of 1989* and *Race to the Sun*, a history of the Paris–Nice race.

Rethinking The Cannibal
by Phil Cavell

I never much cared for The Cannibal nickname. The connotations of voracious greed are too reductive. It was also said that Merckx never left anything on the table for others. Ergo: he ate you and then he ate your lunch. The characterisation is a naive conflation of appetite and greed. The former speaks to motivation and ambition, whilst the latter only to uncontrolled excess. Eddy Merckx was neither greedy nor uncontrolled, as a person or a racer of bicycles. At the end of this essay, I offer a nickname that reflects his qualities more accurately.

Referring to Eddy Merckx as a bike racer is like calling Neil Armstrong a pilot. The real story is they both transcended the moment to encapsulate and then define an epoch. Only geeks remember Michael Collins (*Apollo 11* pilot) and Roger De Vlaeminck (the rival Merckx quietly feared).

Merckx was Elvis, Merckx was Muhammad Ali – men of such unreasonable talent that they distorted the metallic arc of their hour. Hell, Eddy even looked like Elvis.

You can rightfully aim luck and happenstance at Armstrong, Elvis, Merckx, Ali – right place, right time. However, their enduring mythology resides somewhere else. Armstrong flies the Eagle LEM sideways across the surface of the moon, with 1201 and 1202 alarms shrieking in his headset. 1974 – an ageing Ali fears for his life against an infinitely stronger George Foreman. Ali ad-libs rope-a-dope – inviting Big George to punch out his pride on his body. Ali softens the hits as he leans back into the sagging ropes. Round 8 – Ali springs off the ropes to prescribe the minimum force required to fell Big George.

History from hardship.

Contrary to the established mythology, Merckx's super-powers were not his outsized strength or his fathomless desire to win. The Merckx edifice was founded on a granite bedrock of discipline and humility. Eddy Merckx had one-in-a-million genes, honed into an exalted bike-racing phenotype, by great parenting.

Eddy wanted to win races and was fortunate enough to drive the biggest engine in the professional peloton. But he also had the humility to understand that talent wouldn't immunise him against the requirements of training, nutrition and perfectionist preparation.

Prior to 1969, Eddy Merckx was expending the hard hours required to embed the deepest athletic reserves of anyone in the peloton. Unlike some of his peers, he actually relished the exactitude of being a professional bike rider. Merckx never missed training sessions or took short-cuts home. But then… 1969 – Merckx has the kind of crash that ends careers. A freak velodrome accident as he raced behind his Derny rider, Fernand Wambst. It killed Wambst and seriously injured an unconscious Merckx.

Perhaps the years of discipline that Merckx had so assiduously applied to building physical and mental resilience allowed him to cope with the career-deflecting injuries?

But 1969 halted the Merckx production-line of continuous improvement. From here on out are the hard years of body management. Post 1969 Merckx became a world-champion stoic, seeking to hide his pain from those who would seek to profit from it.

Which raises another aspect of Merckx's story. Eddy's objective was uncluttered and clearly stated – he wanted to win any race that he started. Everyone else just wanted to beat Eddy Merckx. He had unwittingly created a new racing paradigm – all roads to victory went through him.

Concentrating on Merckx the man rather than the race, he invited poor judgement and hubris from some of his adversaries – all too easily flooded with glee if he struggled on one climb or on one day – ding-dong the king is dead. He was never dead, just momentarily mortal. Patience and humility are intrinsically linked and Eddy Merckx had a black belt in both.

Merckx is simply one of the greatest athletes that has ever lived, and by some distance, the most consequential bike racer.

The nickname that would have suited him better: The Monk. He devoted himself to the craft like it was a calling. Never lost himself in wealth and fame. His was a quiet and constant reduction to the hard work that would wear others down. Merckx is a story of monastic restraint, not greed.

And to those who would question why Eddy wouldn't give away a race or back off: it would be like asking a monk to stop believing in God.

Chapeau to the man who was dealt a great hand, and then went and played it magnificently for our entertainment.

Phil Cavell is the author of *The Midlife Cyclist.*

Eddy Has The Last Word by Ned Boulting

I came to cycling as a complete outsider, a quarter of a century ago. There were only two bike riders I had ever heard of back then; only two names that had transcended cycling to lodge with the general sporting public. One, unfortunately, was Lance Armstrong. The other was Eddy Merckx.

I was born a couple of weeks before Neil Armstrong landed on the moon in the summer of 1969. By the most fitting of coincidences, this was also the same day on which Eddy Merckx rode to victory in Paris, winning the Tour de France for the first of his five times.

I was very young indeed when Merckx stopped racing, so I certainly can lay no claim to having seen him race on the TV. But somehow that deeply foreign-looking name, with its crush of exotic consonants was woven into the fabric of a 1970s childhood, even in the total cycling backwater that was Britain, far removed from the Flemish and French-speaking heartlands of the sport. Merckx, that one-syllable icon, had migrated successfully across the Channel. His name was inked in print, it crackled over the radio waves, it was announced gravely on TV by men in brown suits, it was stamped on to the frames of racing bikes. We may not have known why he was great. But we knew beyond doubt that he was.

In the summer of 2003, we met for the first time. I ended up walking down the corridor of a two-star hotel somewhere in France, in the same direction, and at the same pace as Eddy Merckx, by now in late middle age, but quite unmistakable. Together we got in a lift and word-lessly descended to the ground floor. As we stood facing the door in silence my heart was thumping, and my only thought was one word: Merckx.

Since that inauspicious start to our relationship, fate has thrown us together on half a dozen occasions. I have hosted him on stage in London, coaxing from him stories of his racing career which he recalled with a straightfor-ward immediacy that put you in the moment with him, placed you alongside him in the blazing heat of the Puy de Dôme, or gliding down the Poggio towards the Via Roma in Sanremo. When talking of his rivals, his brow furrowed minutely, as if to question why they were even in the conversation. Surely we were there to talk of Merckx. What need is there for another name?

Another time, we ate lunch together in Birmingham, while the 2016 Olympics were in progress. His attention was entirely diverted by the fate of the Argentinian hockey team who were playing that afternoon. His grandson was on the team, the son of his daughter who had emigrated. Eddy the hockey fan expressed the same feral intensity as Eddy the greatest rider of all time. There was no compro-mise in his support.

The 2019 Tour started in his honour in his home city of Brussels, 50 years after his moonshot career began. The Grand-Place overflowed with his fellow *Bruxellois*. The sun shone. Eddy stepped out on to the balcony from the shade of the Hôtel de Ville and he raised both arms to salute the crowd.

I will take many memories from my time at the Tour. But that single gesture, simple and complete, will not be forgotten. There will never be another Merckx.

Ned Boulting is the author of *Square Peg, Round Ball, 1923* and *The Accidental Tour-ist*.

At the entrance to the La Cipale velodrome in Vincennes in 1969,
Belgian supporters allow themselves a touch of humor on
a banner: 'Put a MERCKX in your engine'

ACKNOWLEDGEMENTS

I would like to express my gratitude to Robert Janssens, Beppe Conti, Bennie Ceulen and Pascal Sergent. From the beginning to the end of my nine-month journey they supported me with as much generosity as efficiency, and their help was invaluable. And a knowing wink to Jean-Philippe Bouchard, my original publisher, who set me on the track of these glorious forebears. I thank him for that.

Merckx poses with (L to R) Joop Zoetemelk, Gosta Pettersson, Martin Van Den Bossche and Marinus Wagtmans after his second consecutive Tour de France victory

Merckx, out on his own, during the 1969 Tour de France